THIS BOOK BELONGS TO

_____

START DATE

_____

SHE READS TRUTH

EXECUTIVE

FOUNDER/CHIEF EXECUTIVE OFFICER
Raechel Myers

CO-FOUNDER/CHIEF CONTENT OFFICER
Amanda Bible Williams

CHIEF OPERATING OFFICER
Ryan Myers

EDITORIAL

EDITORIAL DIRECTOR
Jessica Lamb

MANAGING EDITOR
Beth Joseph, MDiv

DIGITAL MANAGING EDITOR
Oghosa Iyamu, MDiv

ASSOCIATE EDITORS
Lindsey Jacobi, MDiv
Tameshia Williams, ThM

EDITORIAL ASSISTANT
Hannah Little

MARKETING

**CUSTOMER JOURNEY
MARKETING MANAGER**
Megan Gibbs

PRODUCT MARKETING MANAGER
Wesley Chandler

SOCIAL MEDIA STRATEGIST
Taylor Krupp

CREATIVE

ART DIRECTORS
Kelsea Allen
Aimee Lindamood

DESIGNERS
Abbey Benson
Amanda Brush

JUNIOR DESIGNER
Lauren Haag

LOGISTICS

LOGISTICS DIRECTOR
Lauren Gloyne

PROJECT ASSISTANT
Mary Beth Montgomery

COMMUNITY SUPPORT

COMMUNITY SUPPORT MANAGER
Kara Hewett

COMMUNITY SUPPORT SPECIALISTS
Elise Matson
Katy McKnight
Margot Williams

SHIPPING

SHIPPING MANAGER
Elizabeth Thomas

FULFILLMENT LEAD
Cait Baggerman

FULFILLMENT SPECIALISTS
Ashley Richardson
Noe Sanchez

SUBSCRIPTION INQUIRIES
orders@shereadstruth.com

CONTRIBUTORS

ART
Rebecca Hunter

PHOTOGRAPHY
Amy Lewis (24, 90, 114, 124, 146)

RECIPES
Danielle Walker

SPECIAL THANKS
Neely Tabor

@SHEREADSTRUTH

Download the
She Reads Truth app,
available for iOS
and Android

Subscribe to the
She Reads Truth podcast

SHEREADSTRUTH.COM

SHE READS TRUTH™

© 2022 by She Reads Truth, LLC

All rights reserved.

All photography used by permission.

ISBN 978-1-952670-42-8

1 2 3 4 5 6 7 8 9 10

All Scripture is taken from the Christian Standard Bible®. Copyright © 2020 by Holman Bible Publishers. Used by permission. Christian Standard Bible® and CSB® are federally registered trademarks of Holman Bible Publishers.

Verses omitted in the CSB are also omitted in this book.

"Asparagus Prosciutto Tart," "Blood Orange and Honey," and "Lemon Lavender Bundt Cakes" from DANIELLE WALKER'S AGAINST ALL GRAIN CELEBRATIONS: A YEAR OF GLUTEN-FREE, DAIRY-FREE, AND PALEO RECIPES FOR EVERY OCCASION [A COOKBOOK] by Danielle Walker, copyright © 2016 by Simple Writing Holdings, LLC. Used by permission of Ten Speed Press, an imprint of Random House, a division of Penguin Random House LLC. All rights reserved.

Though the dates in the book have been carefully researched, scholars disagree on the dating of many biblical events.

Research support provided by Logos Bible Software™. Learn more at logos.com.

This book was printed offset in Nashville, Tennessee, on 70# Lynx Opaque. Cover is Neenah Royal Sundance Felt 80#C 100 PC White.

COME TO LIFE

A LENTEN STUDY OF EZEKIEL

SHE READS TRUTH

The message of the cross and
the empty tomb is not just
"Wake up." It's "Come to life!"

Amanda

Amanda Bible Williams
CO-FOUNDER & CHIEF
CONTENT OFFICER

I 've been shopping for an alarm clock, and it is not going well. First of all, there are way too many options. Like everything else in our info-saturated world, alarm clocks have a deep and wide corner of the internet dedicated to them. There is apparently a whole "science of waking," intricately researched theories about every detail—and, unfortunately for me, as many alarm clocks as there are theories.

But the real problem isn't deciding whether to go analog or digital, sunrise or instrumental, woodgrain or acrylic. The problem is why I'm shopping for an alarm clock in the first place: my unhealthy relationship with my smartphone. If this were really just about waking up, any clock would do. But it's more than that. It's about my idols of connection, control, and convenience that demand I keep my phone within reach even while I sleep. I can't settle on the perfect alarm clock because what I'm really looking to solve is not a sleep problem but a heart problem.

I often think of Lent as a season of waking. Numbed by our schedules and scrolling, circumstances and struggles, we intentionally narrow our focus, eliminate distractions, and train our eyes back on the cross, waking up to the life-transforming gospel of Jesus Christ. But the truth is, we need more than a spiritual alarm clock. Scripture teaches that apart from Jesus, we are dead in our sin. The message of the cross and the empty tomb is not just "Wake up." It's "Come to life!"

When the prophet Ezekiel was led by the Spirit of God into the valley of dry bones, the Lord said to him, "Son of man, can these bones live?" The prophet's reply? "Lord GOD, only you know" (Ezekiel 37:3). And he was right. Only God can grant life. And by the finished work of His Son, that is exactly what He has done.

The book of Ezekiel and the Lenten season are invitations to turn to the giver of life and receive what He provides. For these long and beautiful weeks, we will walk to the cross by way of Ezekiel, a book heavy with sin and rich with redemption. We will sit with the exiled prophet and hear God's promise: "I will put breath in you so that you come to life. Then you will know that I am the LORD" (Ezekiel 37:6).

As you read, look for God's presence. Even in the shadows and valleys, He is there. Spend some time with "The Temple in Scripture" extra on page 180—it traces God's dwelling with His people throughout Scripture. And don't miss the sidebar on page 55 that helps us recognize the Holy Spirit's ministry throughout the book. By the power of that same Spirit, may we arrive at Easter Sunday fully awake to the weight and glory of our risen Savior's invitation: Come to life!

At She Reads Truth, we believe in pairing the inherently beautiful Word of God with the aesthetic beauty it deserves. Each of our resources is thoughtfully and artfully designed to highlight the beauty, goodness, and truth of Scripture in a way that reflects the themes of each curated reading plan.

For this Study Book, we used abstract artwork to highlight the imagery in Ezekiel's visions and experiences that are beyond our natural senses, namely the Holy Spirit and the glory of the Lord. Rebecca Hunter's nonrepresentational art reminds us that some of the most important aspects of our faith cannot be perceived with our human senses.

We balanced the abstract imagery in Ezekiel with images of nature for a grounding effect. The use of light in these photos is intentional, pointing to the hope of salvation.

The IvyMode font highlights the contrasts in the book of Ezekiel: a heart of stone versus a heart of flesh, judgment versus redemption, exile versus return. The casual lettering throughout the book adds a personal touch, representing the first-person account likely recorded by the prophet himself rather than an assistant.

Many of the themes in Ezekiel—and the season of Lent—can feel heavy. This is reflected in the book's muted color palette. Themes like lament, sin, and judgment inform the darker tones, while the lighter ones point us to Resurrection Sunday.

"My dwelling place will be with them; I will be their God, and they will be my people."

HOW TO USE THIS BOOK

She Reads Truth is a community of women dedicated to reading the Word of God every day. In this Lenten season we will spend six weeks in the book of Ezekiel, reflecting on the consequences of sin and God's desire for His people to return to Him, followed by Holy Week readings from the Gospels to lead us from Palm Sunday to Easter Sunday.

READ & REFLECT

Your **Come to Life: A Lenten Study of Ezekiel** Study Book focuses primarily on Scripture, with bonus resources to facilitate deeper engagement with God's Word.

SCRIPTURE READING

Designed for a Monday start, this Study Book presents the book of Ezekiel in daily readings, along with additional passages curated to show how themes from the main reading can be found throughout Scripture. The last week focuses on Holy Week.

❦ *Additional passages are marked in your daily reading with the Going Deeper heading.*

REFLECTION

Each weekday features space to note questions as you read, and each week features space for personal reflection and prayer.

COMMUNITY & CONVERSATION

You can start reading this book at any time! If you want to join women from Carson City to Constantinople as they read along with you, the She Reads Truth community will start Day 1 of **Come to Life: A Lenten Study of Ezekiel** on Monday, February 28, 2022.

 ## SHE READS TRUTH APP

Devotionals corresponding to each daily reading can be found in the **Lent 2022: Come to Life** reading plan on the She Reads Truth app. New devotionals will be published each weekday, and each day during Holy Week, once the plan begins on Monday, February 28, 2022. You can use the app to participate in community discussion, download free lock screens for Weekly Truth memorization, and more.

GRACE DAY

Use Saturdays to catch up on your reading, pray, and rest in the presence of the Lord.

WEEKLY TRUTH

Sundays leading up to Holy Week are set aside for Scripture memorization.

See tips for memorizing Scripture on page 236.

EXTRAS

This book features additional tools to help you gain a deeper understanding of the text.

Find a complete list of extras on page 13.

 SHEREADSTRUTH.COM

The **Lent 2022: Come to Life** reading plan and devotionals will also be available at SheReadsTruth.com as the community reads each day. Invite your family, friends, and neighbors to read along with you!

 SHE READS TRUTH PODCAST

Subscribe to the She Reads Truth podcast and join our founders and their guests each week as they talk about the beauty, goodness, and truth they find in Scripture.

 *Podcast episodes 117–123 for our **Lent 2022: Come to Life** series release on Mondays beginning February 28, 2022.*

Table of Contents

WEEK 3

WEEK 4

WEEK 7

HOLY WEEK

EXTRAS

RECIPES

HYMNS

SHE READS EZEKIEL

Key Verse

"I WILL GIVE YOU A NEW HEART AND PUT A NEW SPIRIT WITHIN YOU; I WILL REMOVE YOUR HEART OF STONE AND GIVE YOU A HEART OF FLESH." EZEKIEL 36:26

ON THE TIMELINE

Ezekiel was written during Judah's time of exile in Babylon, about 593 to 571 BC. The last dated oracle in the book occured in the twenty-seventh year of King Jehoiachin (Ezk 29:17), indicating that Ezekiel's ministry lasted twenty-two or twenty-three years. The literary coherence of the book suggests that all editorial work was carried out by a single person, the prophet himself.

A LITTLE BACKGROUND

Ezekiel, son of Buzi, was among the approximately ten thousand citizens of Judah deported to Babylon when King Nebuchadnezzar invaded Jerusalem in 597 BC (2Kg 24:10–17). His prophetic call came four years later, in the fifth year of King Jehoiachin's exile (593 BC). Ezekiel was thirty years old when he received his call (Ezk 1:1), the year he should have begun his duties as a priest in the temple (Nm 4:3). The prophet lived during one of the greatest crises in Israel's history—the destruction of Jerusalem and the temple Ezekiel would have served in as a priest, and the exile of Judah's leading citizens to Babylon.

MESSAGE & PURPOSE

The message of Ezekiel revolves around the fall of Jerusalem in 586 BC. Prior to the announcement of Jerusalem's fall, Ezekiel's message was one of judgment. In this rather scathing review of Israel's history, Ezekiel exposed the nation's moral depravity and absence of spiritual concern (Ezk 2:1–8; 8:7–18; 17:1–21; 20:1–32).

After Jerusalem was destroyed and the nation was in exile, Ezekiel's message became one of hope. God would provide a new heart and a new spirit to enable the people to be faithful and avoid future judgment (Ezk 11:17–20; 36:26–28). The Lord would establish a new temple (Ezk 40–48) and a new way of worship for the people once they were restored.

GIVE THANKS FOR THE BOOK OF EZEKIEL

Though Ezekiel is not often quoted in the New Testament, there are a few notable correlations. The end of Revelation reflects the end of Ezekiel, where the river flows from the presence of God (Ezk 47:1–12; Rv 22:1–6), and Ezekiel's depiction of the return of the exiles as resurrected from the dead is comparable to Paul's concept of regeneration (Eph 2:5). The arrangement of the book—announcing judgment in the beginning and declaring restoration at the end—demonstrates that Ezekiel's message was ultimately one of hope in God's sovereign mercy.

 **TIME TO READ EZEKIEL**
3 hours, 39 minutes

1

In order to discern the meaning of prophetic messages, we should first understand them in their original setting. The prophets delivered God's messages to Israel, Judah, and other ancient Near Eastern societies using relevant historical, geographical, political, and cultural context.

3

God's attributes are wholly present throughout every one of His messages. God is not sometimes loving and sometimes just, nor is there a hierarchy of His traits. He expresses all of His attributes all of the time. Though His unique attributes can be identified separately, His essence remains undivided. When reading passages that emphasize one attribute, remember that all other aspects of who God is also remain true.

2

Books of prophecy are collections of allegories, parables, prose, sermons, oracles, prayers, poetry, and short narrative episodes. These literary works frequently include metaphors, symbolism, and apocalyptic imagery to communicate literal truth. While they are organized into sections and categories, books of prophecy should not be taken as collectively chronological or plot driven, as narrative literature is.

4

The darker prophecy gets, the brighter the cross appears. The bleak imagery of the Old Testament prophets shows that people are without hope apart from a redeemer. Christ went to the cross to atone for the darkest realities described in the prophetic books.

METAPHORS AND ALLEGORIES

Throughout the book of Ezekiel, the prophet delivers God's messages, often using metaphors and allegories for emphasis. Below is a list of what each key metaphor and allegory represents.

JERUSALEM

The useless vine that God throws into the fire as fuel
EZK 15

The unfaithful wife who repeatedly breaks her marriage covenant
EZK 16:1–58

An adulterous daughter, who commits prostitution, along with her sister Samaria
EZK 23

A boiling pot, which will eventually burn up
EZK 24:1–14

JUDAH

A vine that stretches its branches toward two eagles
EZK 17

A lioness whose offspring rule with terror and cruelty
EZK 19:1–9

A vine that is uprooted and thrown to the ground
EZK 19:10–14

TYRE

A ship that wrecks because of its wickedness
EZK 27

PHARAOH, KING OF EGYPT

A mighty cedar tree that will be cut down like Assyria
EZK 31:3–18

EZEKIEL

A watchman for Israel, appointed by God
EZK 33:1–9

ISRAEL'S LEADERS

Unfaithful shepherds who cause the sheep to scatter
EZK 34:1–10

THE LORD

The faithful shepherd who will save His flock
EZK 34:11–24

SIGN ACTS

In addition to using metaphors and allegories, God often instructed Ezekiel to present a visual dramatization of a prophecy, known as a "sign act." Listed below are what each major sign act represented and what God asked Ezekiel to do as a demonstration.

JERUSALEM'S SIEGE AND FALL

EZK 4:1–5:14

Draws Jerusalem on a brick and mimics laying siege to the city

Lies on his left side for 390 days and on his right side for 40 days

Drinks rations of water and eats bread baked over animal excrement

Shaves head and beard; burns a third of the shavings, spreads a third around the city, and scatters a third to the wind

THE EXILE AND ISRAEL'S ANXIETY

EZK 12:1–20

Digs a hole in a wall in the presence of the community and walks through the wall carrying his bags like an exile over his shoulder

Eats bread with trembling and drinks water with anxious shaking

THE ROUTES WHICH NEBUCHADNEZZAR CAN USE TO OVERTAKE THE CITY

EZK 21:18–23

Draws a map and includes a signpost at a fork between two roads, with one road pointing to Rabbah and the other pointing to Jerusalem

THE PEOPLE'S FUTURE RESPONSE TO THE FALL OF THE TEMPLE

EZK 24:15–27

Mourns wife's death privately, refraining from public mourning rituals and customs

THE REUNIFICATION OF THE KINGDOMS OF ISRAEL AND JUDAH

EZK 37:15–28

Writes on two sticks representing the divided kingdoms and then joins them together

The Seasons of the Church

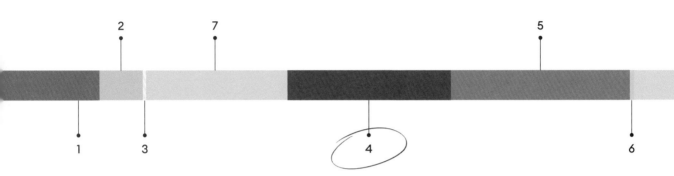

The Lenten season is just one part of the Church calendar, a centuries-old way many Christian denominations order the year to remember and celebrate the redeeming work of Christ. Structured around the moving date of Easter Sunday and the fixed date of Christmas, the liturgical Church calendar consists of six seasons as well as ordinary time.

1

ADVENT

WHAT IS IT?
A season of anticipating the celebration of Jesus's birth, while also anticipating Jesus's promised return. The term *advent* comes from a Latin word meaning "coming" or "arrival."

WHEN IS IT?
Four Sundays before Christmas Day through December 24.

2

CHRISTMASTIDE

WHAT IS IT?
A season celebrating the birth of Jesus.

WHEN IS IT?
December 25 through January 5, also known as the Twelve Days of Christmas and Yuletide.

KEY SCRIPTURES
Is 9:2–7; Mt 1:18–25; Lk 1:26–38; 2:1–20

3

EPIPHANY

WHAT IS IT?
Epiphany comes from a Greek word that means "to manifest" or "to show." It is also known as the Feast of the Three Kings, Three Kings' Day, and Twelfth Night. Epiphany commemorates the arrival of the wise men and is a reminder that Christ's birth is good news for all creation.

WHEN IS IT?
January 6, twelve days after Christmas. Some traditions celebrate this as a season through the Sunday before Ash Wednesday, rather than as just one day.

KEY SCRIPTURE
Mt 2:1–12

7

4

LENT

WHAT IS IT?
A solemn season of
self-reflection, repentance,
and Scripture meditation as a
means of preparing one's heart
and mind to celebrate Easter.

WHEN IS IT?
Ash Wednesday through Holy
Saturday, forty fasting days
and six feasting Sundays.

KEY SCRIPTURE
Lk 4:1–13

5

EASTERTIDE

WHAT IS IT?
A celebration of Jesus Christ's
resurrection, the central
belief of the Christian faith.
Eastertide is the culmination
of Lent.

WHEN IS IT?
Easter Sunday through the day
before Pentecost. At seven
weeks, it is the longest formal
season of the Church year.

KEY SCRIPTURES
Lk 24:1–12, 36–53;
Jn 11:25–26

6

PENTECOST

WHAT IS IT?
A celebration of when the
Holy Spirit descended on
believers from all over the
world who were gathered in
Jerusalem. It marks the birth
of the Christian Church.

WHEN IS IT?
The seventh Sunday
after Easter.

KEY SCRIPTURE
Ac 2:1–41

7

ORDINARY TIME

Most of the Church calendar
consists of ordinary time, the
periods between Pentecost and
Advent, and Epiphany and
Lent. Though the colors used
to mark the other seasons of
the liturgical year differ from
tradition to tradition, ordinary
time is always green.

An Invitation to Lent

For more than a thousand years, Christians around the world have observed the Lenten season with the sober acknowledgment that with humanity came sin; and with sin, came death. As contemporary believers, we are invited—though not required—to do the same.

Scripture tells us that we were made to know God and live in His perfect presence. God formed us from the dust of the earth, declared us to be good, and gave us the honor of bearing His image (Gn 1:27). But in sin, we rebelled against God (Gn 3:1–7). And generations later, we continue to turn away from Him. We fail to obey and fail to seek after Him with our whole hearts. This sin affects not only our own relationship with God, but our relationships with one another and with all of creation—everything is subject to the death, decay, and frustration that comes from sin (Rm 8:20–21).

But God does not leave us in this state. The entire story of Scripture is that of a saving God—one who pursues His people, even after the initial sin in the garden. He invites us to return to Him, to be made new and be part of making all things new (Hs 14:2, 4–7; Zph 3:17). This redemption story culminated in God coming to earth as a man to meet our great need for salvation. Jesus Christ, God the Son, came to deliver us from sin and restore peace and order through His life, death, and resurrection (Jn 3:16–17; Rm 5:1–2).

We are saved by grace through faith, restored to God forever through the sacrifice of Jesus Christ on the cross (Eph 2:1–10). Through the gift of the Holy Spirit, we are invited to play a role in God's redemptive work in the world as we await the day all creation will be perfectly restored.

Lent is a long, slow season. From Ash Wednesday to Holy Saturday, we reflect on our desperate need for salvation before celebrating the miraculous, undeserved gift of Easter Sunday. We remember our need for forgiveness in order to truly rejoice in the unmatched, indescribable way our loving and merciful God meets that need.

DAY 1

WHY READ EZEKIEL
FOR LENT?

The Lenten rhythm of repentance and remembrance is reflected in the story of Ezekiel. In walking through the book of Ezekiel over six weeks, we immerse ourselves in a story of holy judgment, merciful restoration, ever-present hope, and the promise of salvation.

Ezekiel's original audience was a people in peril. They had been taken from their homes into exile in a foreign nation. Their leadership was corrupt, their hearts and worship were directed toward false gods, and their lives were seemingly without hope.

In speech after speech and display after display, the book of Ezekiel portrays the grim reality of sin, using graphic metaphors to grab the attention of both the original audience and readers today. These portrayals are an invitation to wake up to the reality of sin: it is destructive, an evil affront to all that is good and how everything was created to be.

As we read Ezekiel together, notice how deeply sin grieves God, and how deeply sin breaks community and relationship. Take time to acknowledge, lament, and confess your own sin. And do so remembering the completed work of Jesus Christ on your behalf, knowing how this story ends in everlasting life for all those who follow Him.

Ezekiel offers an invitation for us to look into our own hearts, to see what we worship and who we become when left to our own devices. It also points toward the redemption God desires for us, a consistent call to return to abundant life in Him.

Ezekiel reminds us that salvation from God alone is our hope, and the season of Lent and Easter declare that our ultimate hope—Jesus Christ—has already come.

GENESIS 1:27

So God created man
in his own image;
he created him in the image of God;
he created them male and female.

GENESIS 3:1-13

THE TEMPTATION AND THE FALL

[1] Now the serpent was the most cunning of all the wild animals that the Lord God had made. He said to the woman, "Did God really say, 'You can't eat from any tree in the garden'?"

[2] The woman said to the serpent, "We may eat the fruit from the trees in the garden. [3] But about the fruit of the tree in the middle of the garden, God said, 'You must not eat it or touch it, or you will die.'"

[4] "No! You will certainly not die," the serpent said to the woman. [5] "In fact, God knows that when you eat it your eyes will be opened and you will be like God, knowing good and evil." [6] The woman saw that the tree was good for food and delightful to look at, and that it was desirable for obtaining wisdom. So she took some of its fruit and ate it; she also gave some to her husband, who was with her, and he ate it. [7] Then the eyes of both of them were opened, and they knew they were naked; so they sewed fig leaves together and made coverings for themselves.

SIN'S CONSEQUENCES

[8] Then the man and his wife heard the sound of the Lord God walking in the garden at the time of the evening breeze, and they hid from the Lord God among the trees of the garden. [9] So the Lord God called out to the man and said to him, "Where are you?"

[10] And he said, "I heard you in the garden, and I was afraid because I was naked, so I hid."

[11] Then he asked, "Who told you that you were naked? Did you eat from the tree that I commanded you not to eat from?"

[12] The man replied, "The woman you gave to be with me— she gave me some fruit from the tree, and I ate."

[13] So the Lord God asked the woman, "What have you done?"

And the woman said, "The serpent deceived me, and I ate."

EZEKIEL 36:26

"I will give you a new heart and put a new spirit within you; I will remove your heart of stone and give you a heart of flesh."

HOSEA 14:2, 4

[2] Take words of repentance with you
and return to the Lord.
Say to him, "Forgive all our iniquity
and accept what is good,
so that we may repay you
with praise from our lips."

…

[4] "I WILL HEAL THEIR APOSTASY;
I WILL FREELY LOVE THEM,
FOR MY ANGER WILL HAVE TURNED
    FROM HIM."

ZEPHANIAH 3:17

The Lord your God is among you,
a warrior who saves.
He will rejoice over you with gladness.
He will be quiet in his love.
He will delight in you with singing.

JOHN 3:16-17

[16] For God loved the world in this way: He gave his one and only Son, so that everyone who believes in him will not perish but have eternal life. [17] For God did not send his Son into the world to condemn the world, but to save the world through him.

ROMANS 5:1-2

FAITH TRIUMPHS

[1] Therefore, since we have been justified by faith, we have peace with God through our Lord Jesus Christ. [2] We have also obtained access through him by faith into this grace in which we stand, and we boast in the hope of the glory of God.

ROMANS 8:20-21

[20] For the creation was subjected to futility—not willingly, but because of him who subjected it—in the hope [21] that the creation itself will also be set free from the bondage to decay into the glorious freedom of God's children.

EPHESIANS 2:1-10

FROM DEATH TO LIFE

[1] And you were dead in your trespasses and sins [2] in which you previously walked according to the ways of this world, according to the ruler of the power of the air, the spirit now working in the disobedient. [3] We too all previously lived among them in our fleshly desires, carrying out the inclinations of our flesh and thoughts, and we were by nature children under wrath as the others were also. [4] But God, who is rich in mercy, because of his great love that he had for us, [5] made us alive with Christ even though we were dead in trespasses. You are saved by grace! [6] He also raised us up with him and seated us with him in the heavens in Christ Jesus, [7] so that in the coming ages he might display the immeasurable riches of his grace through his kindness to us in Christ Jesus. [8] For you are saved by grace through faith, and this is not from yourselves; it is God's gift— [9] not from works, so that no one can boast. [10] For we are his workmanship, created in Christ Jesus for good works, which God prepared ahead of time for us to do.

Notes

A Vision of the Lord's Glory

DAY 2

EZEKIEL 1

¹ In the thirtieth year, in the fourth month, on the fifth day of the month, while I was among the exiles by the Chebar Canal, the heavens were opened and I saw visions of God.

² On the fifth day of the month—it was the fifth year of King Jehoiachin's exile— ³ the word of the LORD came directly to the priest Ezekiel son of Buzi, in the land of the Chaldeans by the Chebar Canal. The LORD's hand was on him there.

A VISION OF THE LORD'S GLORY

⁴ I looked, and there was a whirlwind coming from the north, a huge cloud with fire flashing back and forth and brilliant light all around it. In the center of the fire, there was a gleam like amber. ⁵ The likeness of four living creatures came from it, and this was their appearance: They looked something like a human, ⁶ but each of them had four faces and four wings. ⁷ Their legs were straight, and the soles of their feet were like the hooves of a calf, sparkling like the gleam of polished bronze. ⁸ They had human hands under their wings on their four sides. All four of them had faces and wings. ⁹ Their wings were touching. The creatures did not turn as they moved; each one went straight ahead. ¹⁰ Their faces looked something like the face of a human, and each of the four had the face of a lion on the right, the face of an ox on the left, and the face of an eagle. ¹¹ That is what their faces were like. Their wings were spread upward; each had two wings touching that of another and two wings covering its body. ¹² Each creature went straight ahead. Wherever the Spirit wanted to go, they went without turning as they moved.

¹³ The likeness of the living creatures was like the appearance of blazing coals of fire or like torches. Fire was moving back and forth between the living creatures; it was bright, with lightning coming out of it. ¹⁴ The creatures were darting back and forth like flashes of lightning.

¹⁵ When I looked at the living creatures, there was one wheel on the ground beside each of the four-faced creatures. ¹⁶ The appearance of the wheels and their craftsmanship was like the gleam of beryl, and all four had the same likeness. Their appearance and craftsmanship was like a wheel within a wheel. ¹⁷ When they moved, they went in any of the four directions, without turning as they moved. ¹⁸ Their four rims were tall and awe-inspiring, completely covered with eyes. ¹⁹ When the living creatures moved, the wheels moved beside them, and when the creatures rose from the earth, the wheels also rose. ²⁰ Wherever the Spirit wanted to go, the creatures went in the direction the Spirit was moving. The wheels rose alongside them, for the spirit of the living creatures was in the wheels. ²¹ When the creatures moved, the wheels moved; when the creatures stopped, the wheels stopped; and when the creatures rose from the earth, the wheels rose alongside them, for the spirit of the living creatures was in the wheels.

SHE READS TRUTH   DAY 2   25

[22] Over the heads of the living creatures the likeness of an expanse was spread out. It gleamed like awe-inspiring crystal, [23] and under the expanse their wings extended one toward another. They each also had two wings covering their bodies. [24] When they moved, I heard the sound of their wings like the roar of a huge torrent, like the voice of the Almighty, and a sound of tumult like the noise of an army. When they stopped, they lowered their wings.

[25] A voice came from above the expanse over their heads; when they stopped, they lowered their wings. [26] Something like a throne with the appearance of lapis lazuli was above the expanse over their heads. On the throne, high above, was someone who looked like a human. [27] From what seemed to be his waist up, I saw a gleam like amber, with what looked like fire enclosing it all around. From what seemed to be his waist down, I also saw what looked like fire. There was a brilliant light all around him. [28] The appearance of the brilliant light all around was like that of a rainbow in a cloud on a rainy day. This was the appearance of the likeness of the Lord's glory. When I saw it, I fell facedown and heard a voice speaking.

EZEKIEL 2

MISSION TO REBELLIOUS ISRAEL

[1] He said to me, "Son of man, stand up on your feet and I will speak with you." [2] As he spoke to me, the Spirit entered me and set me on my feet, and I listened to the one who was speaking to me. [3] He said to me, "Son of man, I am sending you to the Israelites, to the rebellious pagans who have rebelled against me. The Israelites and their ancestors have transgressed against me to this day. [4] The descendants are obstinate and hardhearted. I am sending you to them, and you must say to them, 'This is what the Lord God says.' [5] Whether they listen or refuse to listen—for they are a rebellious house—they will know that a prophet has been among them.

[6] "But you, son of man, do not be afraid of them and do not be afraid of their words, even though briers and thorns are beside you and you live among scorpions. Don't be afraid of their words or discouraged by the look on their faces, for they are a rebellious house.

[7] SPEAK MY WORDS TO THEM WHETHER THEY LISTEN OR REFUSE TO LISTEN, FOR THEY ARE REBELLIOUS.

[8] "And you, son of man, listen to what I tell you: Do not be rebellious like that rebellious house. Open your mouth and eat what I am giving you." [9] So I looked and saw a hand reaching out to me, and there was a written scroll in it. [10] When he unrolled it before me, it was written on the front and back; words of lamentation, mourning, and woe were written on it.

Notes

REVELATION 4

THE THRONE ROOM OF HEAVEN

¹ After this I looked, and there in heaven was an open door. The first voice that I had heard speaking to me like a trumpet said, "Come up here, and I will show you what must take place after this."

² Immediately I was in the Spirit, and there was a throne in heaven and someone was seated on it. ³ The one seated there had the appearance of jasper and carnelian stone. A rainbow that had the appearance of an emerald surrounded the throne.

⁴ Around the throne were twenty-four thrones, and on the thrones sat twenty-four elders dressed in white clothes, with golden crowns on their heads.

⁵ Flashes of lightning and rumblings and peals of thunder came from the throne. Seven fiery torches were burning before the throne, which are the seven spirits of God. ⁶ Something like a sea of glass, similar to crystal, was also before the throne.

Four living creatures covered with eyes in front and in back were around the throne on each side. ⁷ The first living creature was like a lion; the second living creature was like an ox; the third living creature had a face like a man; and the fourth living creature was like a flying eagle. ⁸ Each of the four living creatures had six wings; they were covered with eyes around and inside. Day and night they never stop, saying,

> Holy, holy, holy,
> Lord God, the Almighty,
> who was, who is, and who is to come.

⁹ Whenever the living creatures give glory, honor, and thanks to the one seated on the throne, the one who lives forever and ever, ¹⁰ the twenty-four elders fall down before the one seated on the throne and worship the one who lives forever and ever. They cast their crowns before the throne and say,

> ¹¹ Our Lord and God,
> you are worthy to receive
> glory and honor and power,
> because you have created all things,
> and by your will
> they exist and were created.

"Son of man, I have made you a watchman over the house of Israel."

EZEKIEL 3:17

Ezekiel As a Watchman

EZEKIEL 3

¹ He said to me, "Son of man, eat what you find here. Eat this scroll, then go and speak to the house of Israel." ² So I opened my mouth, and he fed me the scroll. ³ "Son of man," he said to me, "feed your stomach and fill your belly with this scroll I am giving you." So I ate it, and it was as sweet as honey in my mouth.

⁴ Then he said to me, "Son of man, go to the house of Israel and speak my words to them. ⁵ For you are not being sent to a people of unintelligible speech or a difficult language but to the house of Israel— ⁶ not to the many peoples of unintelligible speech or a difficult language, whose words you cannot understand. No doubt, if I sent you to them, they would listen to you. ⁷ But the house of Israel will not want to listen to you because they do not want to listen to me. For the whole house of Israel is hardheaded and hardhearted. ⁸ Look, I have made your face as hard as their faces and your forehead as hard as their foreheads. ⁹ I have made your forehead like a diamond, harder than flint. Don't be afraid of them or discouraged by the look on their faces, though they are a rebellious house."

¹⁰ Next he said to me, "Son of man, listen carefully to all my words that I speak to you and take them to heart. ¹¹ Go to your people, the exiles, and speak to them. Tell them, 'This is what the Lord God says,' whether they listen or refuse to listen."

¹² The Spirit then lifted me up, and I heard a loud rumbling sound behind me—bless the glory of the Lord in his place!— ¹³ with the sound of the living creatures' wings brushing against each other and the sound of the wheels beside them, a loud rumbling sound. ¹⁴ The Spirit lifted me up and took me away. I left in bitterness and in an angry spirit, and the Lord's hand was on me powerfully. ¹⁵ I came to the exiles at Tel-abib, who were living by the Chebar Canal, and I sat there among them stunned for seven days.

EZEKIEL AS A WATCHMAN

¹⁶ Now at the end of seven days the word of the Lord came to me: ¹⁷ "Son of man, I have made you a watchman over the house of Israel. When you hear a word from my mouth, give them a warning from me. ¹⁸ If I say to the wicked person, 'You will surely die,' but you do not warn him—you don't speak out to warn him about his wicked way in order to save his life—that wicked person will die for his iniquity. Yet I will hold you responsible for his blood. ¹⁹ But if you warn a wicked person and he does not turn from his wickedness or his wicked way, he will die for his iniquity, but you will have rescued yourself. ²⁰ Now if a righteous person turns from his righteousness and acts unjustly, and I put a stumbling block in front of him, he will die. If you did not warn him, he will die because of his sin, and the righteous acts he did will not be remembered. Yet I will hold you responsible for his

blood. ²¹ But if you warn the righteous person that he should not sin, and he does not sin, he will indeed live because he listened to your warning, and you will have rescued yourself."

²² The hand of the LORD was on me there, and he said to me, "Get up, go out to the plain, and I will speak with you there." ²³ So I got up and went out to the plain. The LORD's glory was present there, like the glory I had seen by the Chebar Canal, and I fell facedown. ²⁴ The Spirit entered me and set me on my feet. He spoke with me and said, "Go, shut yourself inside your house. ²⁵ As for you, son of man, they will put ropes on you and bind you with them so you cannot go out among them. ²⁶ I will make your tongue stick to the roof of your mouth, and you will be mute and unable to be a mediator for them, for they are a rebellious house. ²⁷ But when I speak with you, I will open your mouth, and you will say to them, 'This is what the Lord GOD says.' Let the one who listens, listen, and let the one who refuses, refuse—for they are a rebellious house."

◗ GOING DEEPER

ISAIAH 6

ISAIAH'S CALL AND MISSION

¹ In the year that King Uzziah died, I saw the Lord seated on a high and lofty throne, and the hem of his robe filled the temple. ² Seraphim were standing above him; they each had six wings: with two they covered their faces, with two they covered their feet, and with two they flew. ³ And one called to another:

Holy, holy, holy is the LORD of Armies;
his glory fills the whole earth.

⁴ The foundations of the doorways shook at the sound of their voices, and the temple was filled with smoke.

⁵ Then I said:

Woe is me for I am ruined
because I am a man of unclean lips
and live among a people of unclean lips,

and because my eyes have seen the King,
the LORD of Armies.

⁶ Then one of the seraphim flew to me, and in his hand was a glowing coal that he had taken from the altar with tongs. ⁷ He touched my mouth with it and said:

Now that this has touched your lips,
your iniquity is removed
and your sin is atoned for.

⁸ Then I heard the voice of the Lord asking:

Who will I send?
Who will go for us?

I said:

Here I am. Send me.

⁹ And he replied:

Go! Say to these people:
Keep listening, but do not understand;
keep looking, but do not perceive.
¹⁰ Make the minds of these people dull;
deafen their ears and blind their eyes;
otherwise they might see with their eyes
and hear with their ears,
understand with their minds,
turn back, and be healed.

¹¹ Then I said, "Until when, Lord?" And he replied:

Until cities lie in ruins without inhabitants,
houses are without people,
the land is ruined and desolate,
¹² and the LORD drives the people far away,
leaving great emptiness in the land.
¹³ Though a tenth will remain in the land,
it will be burned again.
Like the terebinth or the oak
that leaves a stump when felled,
the holy seed is the stump.

Notes

Ezekiel Dramatizes Jerusalem's Fall

DAY 4

JERUSALEM'S SIEGE DRAMATIZED

¹ "Now you, son of man, take a brick, set it in front of you, and draw the city of Jerusalem on it. ² Then lay siege against it: Construct a siege wall, build a ramp, pitch military camps, and place battering rams against it on all sides. ³ Take an iron plate and set it up as an iron wall between yourself and the city. Face it so that it is under siege, and besiege it. This will be a sign for the house of Israel.

⁴ "Then lie down on your left side and place the iniquity of the house of Israel on it. You will bear their iniquity for the number of days you lie on your side. ⁵ For I have assigned you the years of their iniquity according to the number of days you lie down, 390 days; so you will bear the iniquity of the house of Israel. ⁶ When you have completed these days, lie down again, but on your right side, and bear the iniquity of the house of Judah. I have assigned you forty days, a day for each year. ⁷ Face the siege of Jerusalem with your arm bared, and prophesy against it. ⁸ Be aware that I will put cords on you so you cannot turn from side to side until you have finished the days of your siege.

⁹ "Also take wheat, barley, beans, lentils, millet, and spelt. Put them in a single container and make them into bread for yourself. You are to eat it during the number of days you lie on your side, 390 days. ¹⁰ The food you eat each day will weigh eight ounces; you will eat it at set times. ¹¹ You will also drink a ration of water, a sixth of a gallon, which you will drink at set times. ¹² You will eat it as you would a barley cake and bake it over dried human excrement in their sight." ¹³ The LORD said, "This is how the Israelites will eat their bread—ceremonially unclean—among the nations where I will banish them."

¹⁴ But I said, "Oh, Lord GOD, I have never been defiled. From my youth until now I have not eaten anything that died naturally or was mauled by wild beasts. And impure meat has never entered my mouth."

¹⁵ He replied to me, "Look, I will let you use cow dung instead of human excrement, and you can make your bread over that." ¹⁶ He said to me, "Son of man, I am going to

cut off the supply of bread in Jerusalem. They will anxiously eat food they have weighed out and in dread drink rationed water [17] for lack of bread and water. Everyone will be devastated and waste away because of their iniquity."

EZEKIEL 5

EZEKIEL DRAMATIZES JERUSALEM'S FALL

[1] "Now you, son of man, take a sharp sword, use it as you would a barber's razor, and shave your head and beard. Then take a set of scales and divide the hair. [2] You are to burn a third of it in the city when the days of the siege have ended; you are to take a third and slash it with the sword all around the city; and you are to scatter a third to the wind, for I will draw a sword to chase after them. [3] But you are to take a few strands from the hair and secure them in the folds of your robe. [4] Take some more of them, throw them into the fire, and burn them in it. A fire will spread from it to the whole house of Israel.

[5] "This is what the Lord God says:

I HAVE SET THIS JERUSALEM IN THE CENTER OF THE NATIONS,

with countries all around her. [6] She has rebelled against my ordinances with more wickedness than the nations, and against my statutes more than the countries that surround her. For her people have rejected my ordinances and have not walked in my statutes.

[7] "Therefore, this is what the Lord God says: Because you have been more insubordinate than the nations around you—you have not walked in my statutes or kept my ordinances; you have not even kept the ordinances of the nations around you— [8] therefore, this is what the Lord God says: See, I myself am against you, Jerusalem, and I will execute judgments within you in the sight of the nations. [9] Because of all your detestable practices, I will do to you what I have never done before and what I will never do again. [10] As a result, fathers will eat their sons within Jerusalem, and sons will eat their fathers. I will execute judgments against you and scatter all your survivors to every direction of the wind.

[11] "Therefore, as I live"—this is the declaration of the Lord God—"I will withdraw and show you no pity, because you have defiled my sanctuary with all your abhorrent acts and detestable practices. Yes, I will not spare you. [12] A third of your people will die by plague and be consumed by famine within you; a third will fall by the sword all around you; and I will scatter a third to every direction of the wind, and I will draw a sword to chase after them. [13] When my anger is spent and I have vented my wrath on them, I will be appeased. Then after I have spent my wrath on them, they will know that I, the Lord, have spoken in my jealousy.

Notes

God gone detailed instructions

[14] "I will make you a ruin and a disgrace among the nations around you, in the sight of everyone who passes by. [15] So you will be a disgrace and a taunt, a warning and a horror, to the nations around you when I execute judgments against you in anger, wrath, and furious rebukes. I, the LORD, have spoken. [16] When I shoot deadly arrows of famine at them, arrows for destruction that I will send to destroy you, inhabitants of Jerusalem, I will intensify the famine against you and cut off your supply of bread. [17] I will send famine and dangerous animals against you. They will leave you childless. Plague and bloodshed will sweep through you, and I will bring a sword against you. I, the LORD, have spoken."

GOING DEEPER

ISAIAH 26:8–9

[8] Yes, LORD, we wait for you
in the path of your judgments.
Our desire is for your name and renown.
[9] I long for you in the night;
yes, my spirit within me diligently seeks you,
for when your judgments are in the land,
the inhabitants of the world will learn righteousness.

1 PETER 2:24

He himself bore our sins in his body on the tree; so that, having died to sins, we might live for righteousness. By his wounds you have been healed.

Notes

"Yet I will leave a remnant when you

are scattered among the nations..."

EZEKIEL 6:8

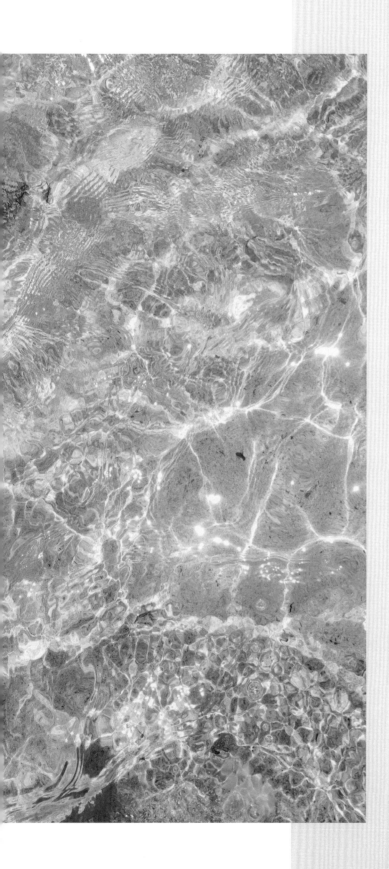

A Lament Over the Fall of Jerusalem

5

EZEKIEL 6

A PROPHECY AGAINST ISRAEL'S IDOLATRY

[1] The word of the LORD came to me: [2] "Son of man, face the mountains of Israel and prophesy against them. [3] You are to say: Mountains of Israel, hear the word of the Lord GOD! This is what the Lord GOD says to the mountains and the hills, to the ravines and the valleys: I am about to bring a sword against you, and I will destroy your high places. [4] Your altars will be desolated and your shrines smashed. I will throw down your slain in front of your idols. [5] I will lay the corpses of the Israelites in front of their idols and scatter your bones around your altars. [6] Wherever you live the cities will be in ruins and the high places will be desolate, so that your altars will lie in ruins and be desecrated, your idols smashed and obliterated, your shrines cut down, and what you have made wiped out. [7] The slain will fall among you, and you will know that I am the LORD.

[8] "Yet I will leave a remnant when you are scattered among the nations, for throughout the countries there will be some of you who will escape the sword. [9] Then your survivors will remember me among the nations where they are taken captive, how I was crushed by their promiscuous hearts that turned away from me and by their eyes that lusted after their idols. They will loathe themselves because of the evil things they did, their detestable actions of every kind. [10] And they will know that I am the LORD; I did not threaten to bring this disaster on them without a reason.

LAMENT OVER THE FALL OF JERUSALEM

[11] "This is what the Lord GOD says: Clap your hands, stamp your feet, and cry out over all the evil and detestable practices of the house of Israel, who will fall by the sword, famine, and plague. [12] The one who is far off will die by plague; the one who is near will fall by the sword; and the one who remains and is spared will die of famine. In this way I will exhaust my wrath on them. [13] You will all know that I am the LORD when their slain lie among their idols around their altars, on every high hill, on all the mountaintops, and under every green tree and every leafy oak—the places where they offered pleasing aromas to all their idols. [14] I will stretch out my hand against them, and wherever they live I will make the land a desolate waste, from the wilderness to Riblah. Then they will know that I am the LORD."

EZEKIEL 7

ANNOUNCEMENT OF THE END

[1] The word of the LORD came to me: [2] "Son of man, this is what the Lord GOD says to the land of Israel:

An end! The end has come
on the four corners of the earth.
[3] The end is now upon you;
I will send my anger against you
and judge you according to your ways.
I will punish you for all your detestable practices.
[4] I will not look on you with pity or spare you,
but I will punish you for your ways
and for your detestable practices within you.
Then you will know that I am the LORD."

[5] This is what the Lord GOD says:

Look, one disaster after another is coming!
[6] An end has come; the end has come!
It has awakened against you.
Look, it is coming!
[7] Doom has come on you,
inhabitants of the land.
The time has come; the day is near.
There will be panic on the mountains
and not celebration.

[8] I will pour out my wrath on you very soon;
I will exhaust my anger against you
and judge you according to your ways.
I will punish you for all your detestable practices.
[9] I will not look on you with pity or spare you.
I will punish you for your ways
and for your detestable practices within you.
Then you will know
that it is I, the LORD, who strikes.

[10] Here is the day! Here it comes!
Doom is on its way.
The rod has blossomed;
arrogance has bloomed.
[11] Violence has grown into a rod of wickedness.
None of them will remain:

none of that crowd,
none of their wealth,
and none of the eminent among them.

[12] The time has come; the day has arrived.
Let the buyer not rejoice
and the seller not mourn,
for wrath is on her whole crowd.
[13] The seller will certainly not return
to what was sold
as long as he and the buyer remain alive.
For the vision concerning her whole crowd
will not be revoked,
and because of the iniquity of each one,
none will preserve his life.

[14] They have blown the trumpet
and prepared everything,
but no one goes to war,
for my wrath is on her whole crowd.
[15] The sword is on the outside;
plague and famine are on the inside.
Whoever is in the field will die by the sword,
and famine and plague will devour
whoever is in the city.

[16] The survivors among them will escape
and live on the mountains.
Like doves of the valley,
all of them will moan,
each over his own iniquity.
[17] All their hands will become weak,
and all their knees will run with urine.
[18] They will put on sackcloth,
and horror will overwhelm them.
Shame will cover all their faces,
and all their heads will be bald.

[19] They will throw their silver into the streets,
and their gold will seem like something filthy.
Their silver and gold will be unable to save them
in the day of the LORD's wrath.
They will not satisfy their appetites
or fill their stomachs,

for these were the stumbling blocks
that brought about their iniquity.

[20] He appointed his beautiful ornaments for majesty,
but they made their detestable images from them,
their abhorrent things.
Therefore, I have made these
into something filthy to them.
[21] I will hand these things over
to foreigners as plunder
and to the wicked of the earth as spoil,
and they will profane them.
[22] I will turn my face from them
as they profane my treasured place.
Violent men will enter it and profane it.

[23] Forge the chain,
for the land is filled with crimes of bloodshed,
and the city is filled with violence.
[24] So I will bring the most evil of nations
to take possession of their houses.
I will put an end to the pride of the strong,
and their sacred places will be profaned.
[25] Anguish is coming!
They will look for peace, but there will be none.
[26] Disaster after disaster will come,
and there will be rumor after rumor.
Then they will look for a vision from a prophet,
but instruction will perish from the priests
and counsel from the elders.
[27] The king will mourn;
the prince will be clothed in grief;
and the hands of the people of the land will tremble.
I will deal with them according to their own conduct,
and I will judge them by their own standards.
Then they will know that I am the LORD.

🕮 GOING DEEPER

GALATIANS 6:7-9

[7] Don't be deceived: God is not mocked. For whatever a person sows he will also reap, [8] because the one who sows to

his flesh will reap destruction from the flesh, but the one who sows to the Spirit will reap eternal life from the Spirit.

9 LET US NOT GET TIRED OF DOING GOOD, FOR WE WILL REAP AT THE PROPER TIME IF WE DON'T GIVE UP.

JAMES 4:1-6

PROUD OR HUMBLE

1 What is the source of wars and fights among you? Don't they come from your passions that wage war within you? 2 You desire and do not have. You murder and covet and cannot obtain. You fight and wage war. You do not have because you do not ask. 3 You ask and don't receive because you ask with wrong motives, so that you may spend it on your pleasures.

4 You adulterous people! Don't you know that friendship with the world is hostility toward God? So whoever wants to be the friend of the world becomes the enemy of God. 5 Or do you think it's without reason that the Scripture says: The spirit he made to dwell in us envies intensely?

6 But he gives greater grace. Therefore he says:

God resists the proud
but gives grace to the humble.

Response

In Scripture, lament is a form of Hebrew poetry that expresses grief or sorrow. God's people have often used lament to petition God for various reasons: deliverance from suffering, wisdom in how to endure pain, grief over sin, and sorrow from loss. Throughout the book of Ezekiel, different moments occur where Ezekiel laments (see Ezekiel 19 and 27). Ezekiel grieves over how many have lost sight of the holiness of God and have forgotten the seriousness of sin and its effects. In lament, we grieve our individual sin, but we also reflect on how our sin affects others.

LAMENT

During this Lenten season, we make time to lament— to grieve our own sin and express sorrow over the brokenness of the world, to which our sin contributes.

1 What in your life do you need to lament? Take time to confess your own sin and grieve over how the sin of others has affected you.

2 How does your sin and brokenness affect your community? Take time to lament for the brokenness you see in the world.

CONFESSION
AND ASSURANCE

A lament is not a quick
fix, but God is faithful,
and lamenting gently but
persistently reminds us to
trust Him. Use this space to
confess your need for God
and His intervention, as well
as express your continued
hope found in His provision.

Come, Ye Sinners, Poor and Needy

WORDS
Joseph Hart; refrain, anonymous

MUSIC
Walker's *Southern Harmony*

1. Come, ye sin-ners, poor and need-y, Weak and wound-ed, sick and sore;
2. Come, ye thirst-y, come, and wel-come, God's free bount-y glo-ri-fy;
3. Come, ye wea-ry, heav-y-la-den, Lost and ru-ined by the fall;
4. Let not con-science make you lin-ger, Nor of fit-ness fond-ly dream;

Je-sus read-y stands to save you, Full of pit-y, love, and pow'r.
True be-lief and true re-pen-tance, Ev-'ry grace that brings you nigh.
If you tar-ry till you're bet-ter, You will nev-er come at all.
All the fit-ness He re-quir-eth is to feel your need of Him.

Chorus

I will a-rise and go to Je-sus, He will em-brace me in His arms;

In the arms of my dear Sav-ior, O there are ten thou-sand charms.

GRACE DAY

He himself bore our sins in his body on the tree; so that, having died to sins, we might live for righteousness. By his wounds you have been healed.

1 PETER 2:24

DAY 6

Lent is a season where we reflect on the depth of our sin and embrace the hope and strength found only in the cross of Christ. We seek unhurried moments of quiet to read Scripture, pray, confess, and repent. Take some time today to catch up on your reading, make space for prayer, and rest in God's presence.

Rebecca Hunter, *A Promise*, 2020, oil on canvas, 48x60 in.

7

Weekly Truth

Scripture is God-breathed and true. When we memorize it, we carry His Word with us wherever we go.

The book of Ezekiel is part of our larger redemption story. As we read it, we will memorize Ezekiel 36:26–28, where God promises to restore Israel after they have experienced His judgment. This week we will begin by memorizing the first part of verse 26.

"I will give you a new heart and put a new spirit within you; I will remove your heart of stone and give you a heart of flesh. I will place my Spirit within you and cause you to follow my statutes and carefully observe my ordinances. You will live in the land that I gave your ancestors; you will be my people, and I will be your God."

EZEKIEL 36:26–28

See tips for memorizing Scripture on page 236.

I SAW THE GLORY OF THE GOD OF ISRAEL THERE, LIKE THE VISION I HAD SEEN IN THE PLAIN. EZEKIEL 8:4

A Visionary Journey to Jerusalem

EZEKIEL 8

A VISIONARY JOURNEY TO JERUSALEM

¹ In the sixth year, in the sixth month, on the fifth day of the month, I was sitting in my house and the elders of Judah were sitting in front of me, and there the hand of the Lord GOD came down on me. ² I looked, and there was someone who looked like a man. From what seemed to be his waist down was fire, and from his waist up was something that looked bright, like the gleam of amber. ³ He stretched out what appeared to be a hand and took me by the hair of my head.

THEN THE SPIRIT LIFTED ME UP BETWEEN EARTH AND HEAVEN AND CARRIED ME IN VISIONS OF GOD TO JERUSALEM,

to the entrance of the inner gate that faces north, where the offensive statue that provokes jealousy was located. ⁴ I saw the glory of the God of Israel there, like the vision I had seen in the plain.

PAGAN PRACTICES IN THE TEMPLE

⁵ The LORD said to me, "Son of man, look toward the north." I looked to the north, and there was this offensive statue north of the Altar Gate, at the entrance. ⁶ He said to me, "Son of man, do you see what they are doing here—more detestable acts that the house of Israel is committing—

so that I must depart from my sanctuary? You will see even more detestable acts."

⁷ Then he brought me to the entrance of the court, and when I looked there was a hole in the wall. ⁸ He said to me, "Son of man, dig through the wall." So I dug through the wall and discovered a doorway. ⁹ He said to me, "Go in and see the detestable, wicked acts they are committing here."

¹⁰ I went in and looked, and there engraved all around the wall was every kind of abhorrent thing—crawling creatures and beasts—as well as all the idols of the house of Israel. ¹¹ Seventy elders from the house of Israel were standing before them, with Jaazaniah son of Shaphan standing among them. Each had a firepan in his hand, and a fragrant cloud of incense was rising up. ¹² He said to me, "Son of man, do you see what the elders of the house of Israel are doing in the darkness, each at the shrine of his idol? For they are saying, 'The LORD does not see us. The LORD has abandoned the land.'" ¹³ Again he said to me, "You will see even more detestable acts that they are committing."

¹⁴ Then he brought me to the entrance of the north gate of the LORD's house, and I saw women sitting there weeping for

Tammuz. [15] And he said to me, "Do you see this, son of man? You will see even more detestable acts than these."

[16] So he brought me to the inner court of the Lord's house, and there were about twenty-five men at the entrance of the Lord's temple, between the portico and the altar, with their backs to the Lord's temple and their faces turned to the east. They were bowing to the east in worship of the sun. [17] And he said to me, "Do you see this, son of man? Is it not enough for the house of Judah to commit the detestable acts they are doing here, that they must also fill the land with violence and repeatedly anger me, even putting the branch to their nose? [18] Therefore I will respond with wrath. I will not show pity or spare them. Though they call loudly in my hearing, I will not listen to them."

EZEKIEL 9

VISION OF SLAUGHTER IN JERUSALEM

[1] Then he called loudly in my hearing, "Come near, executioners of the city, each of you with a destructive weapon in his hand." [2] And I saw six men coming from the direction of the Upper Gate, which faces north, each with a war club in his hand. There was another man among them, clothed in linen, carrying writing equipment. They came and stood beside the bronze altar.

[3] Then the glory of the God of Israel rose from above the cherub where it had been, to the threshold of the temple. He called to the man clothed in linen and carrying writing equipment. [4] "Pass throughout the city of Jerusalem," the Lord said to him, "and put a mark on the foreheads of the men who sigh and groan over all the detestable practices committed in it."

[5] He spoke to the others in my hearing: "Pass through the city after him and start killing; do not show pity or spare them! [6] Slaughter the old men, the young men and women, as well as the children and older women, but do not come near anyone who has the mark. Begin at my sanctuary." So they began with the elders who were in front of the temple. [7] Then he said to them, "Defile the temple and fill the courts with the slain. Go!" So they went out killing people in the city.

[8] While they were killing, I was left alone. And I fell facedown and cried out, "Oh, Lord God! Are you going to destroy the entire remnant of Israel when you pour out your wrath on Jerusalem?"

[9] He answered me, "The iniquity of the house of Israel and Judah is extremely great; the land is full of bloodshed, and the city full of perversity. For they say, 'The Lord has abandoned the land; he does not see.' [10] But as for me, I will not show pity or spare them. I will bring their conduct down on their own heads."

[11] Then the man clothed in linen and carrying writing equipment reported back, "I have done all that you commanded me."

Notes

🔖 GOING DEEPER

ISAIAH 26:20-21

[20] Go, my people, enter your rooms
and close your doors behind you.
Hide for a little while until the wrath has passed.
[21] For look, the LORD is coming from his place
to punish the inhabitants of the earth for their iniquity.
The earth will reveal the blood shed on it
and will no longer conceal her slain.

REVELATION 7:1-3

THE SEALED OF ISRAEL

[1] After this I saw four angels standing at the four corners of the earth, restraining the four winds of the earth so that no wind could blow on the earth or on the sea or on any tree. [2] Then I saw another angel rising up from the east, who had the seal of the living God. He cried out in a loud voice to the four angels who were allowed to harm the earth and the sea, [3] "Don't harm the earth or the sea or the trees until we seal the servants of our God on their foreheads."

Protection for those who have not turned from God to idols

For those who did not trust in idols

God's Glory Leaves the Temple

EZEKIEL 10

GOD'S GLORY LEAVES THE TEMPLE

[1] Then I looked, and there above the expanse over the heads of the cherubim was something like a throne with the appearance of lapis lazuli. [2] The LORD spoke to the man clothed in linen and said, "Go inside the wheelwork beneath the cherubim. Fill your hands with blazing coals from among the cherubim and scatter them over the city." So he went in as I watched.

[3] Now the cherubim were standing to the south of the temple when the man went in, and the cloud filled the inner court. [4] Then the glory of the LORD rose from above the cherub to the threshold of the temple. The temple was filled with the cloud, and the court was filled with the brightness of the LORD's glory. [5] The sound of the cherubim's wings could be heard as far as the outer court; it was like the voice of God Almighty when he speaks.

[6] After the LORD commanded the man clothed in linen, saying, "Take fire from inside the wheelwork, from among the cherubim," the man went in and stood beside a wheel. [7] Then the cherub reached out his hand to the fire that was among them. He took some and put it into the hands of the man clothed in linen, who took it and went out. [8] The cherubim appeared to have the form of human hands under their wings.

[9] I LOOKED, AND THERE WERE FOUR WHEELS BESIDE THE CHERUBIM, ONE WHEEL BESIDE EACH CHERUB.

The luster of the wheels was like the gleam of beryl. [10] In appearance, all four looked alike, like a wheel within a wheel. [11] When they moved, they would go in any of the four directions, without pivoting as they moved. But wherever the head faced, they would go in that direction, without pivoting as they went. [12] Their entire bodies, including their backs, hands, wings, and the wheels that the four of them had, were full of eyes all around. [13] As I listened the wheels were called "the wheelwork." [14] Each one had four faces: one was the face of a cherub, the second the face of a human, the third the face of a lion, and the fourth the face of an eagle.

[15] The cherubim ascended; these were the living creatures I had seen by the Chebar Canal. [16] When the cherubim moved, the wheels moved beside them, and when they lifted their wings to rise from the earth, even then the wheels did not veer away from them. [17] When the cherubim stopped, the wheels stood still, and when they ascended, the wheels ascended with them, for the spirit of the living creatures was in them.

54   COME TO LIFE: A LENTEN STUDY OF EZEKIEL

¹⁸ Then the glory of the LORD moved away from the threshold of the temple and stopped above the cherubim. ¹⁹ The cherubim lifted their wings and ascended from the earth right before my eyes; the wheels were beside them as they went. The glory of the God of Israel was above them, and it stopped at the entrance to the eastern gate of the LORD's house.

²⁰ These were the living creatures I had seen beneath the God of Israel by the Chebar Canal, and I recognized that they were cherubim. ²¹ Each had four faces and each had four wings, with what looked something like human hands under their wings. ²² Their faces looked like the same faces I had seen by the Chebar Canal. Each creature went straight ahead.

EZEKIEL 11:1–13

VISION OF ISRAEL'S CORRUPT LEADERS

¹ The Spirit then lifted me up and brought me to the eastern gate of the LORD's house, which faces east, and at the gate's entrance were twenty-five men. Among them I saw Jaazaniah son of Azzur, and Pelatiah son of Benaiah, leaders of the people. ² The LORD said to me, "Son of man, these are the men who plot evil and give wicked advice in this city. ³ They are saying, 'Isn't the time near to build houses? The city is the pot, and we are the meat.' ⁴ Therefore, prophesy against them. Prophesy, son of man!"

⁵ Then the Spirit of the LORD came on me, and he told me, "You are to say, 'This is what the LORD says: That is what you are thinking, house of Israel; and I know the thoughts that arise in your mind. ⁶ You have multiplied your slain in this city, filling its streets with them.

⁷ "'Therefore, this is what the Lord GOD says: The slain you have put within it are the meat, and the city is the pot, but I will take you out of it. ⁸ You fear the sword, so I will bring the sword against you. This is the declaration of the Lord GOD. ⁹ I will take you out of the city and hand you over to foreigners; I will execute judgments against you. ¹⁰ You will fall by the sword, and I will judge you at the border of Israel. Then you will know that I am the LORD. ¹¹ The city will not be a pot for you, and you will not be the meat within it. I will judge you at the border of Israel, ¹² so you will know that I am the LORD, whose statutes you have not followed and

THE HOLY SPIRIT IN EZEKIEL

There are fifty-two uses of the Hebrew word *ruah*, translated "spirit" or "wind," in Ezekiel. Because of this, Ezekiel has been referred to as the prophet of the Spirit.

As you read, notice how the prophet's ministry is greatly influenced by the movement of the Holy Spirit. Ezekiel's many encounters give us insight into the work and ministry of the Spirit. Below are some examples of the Spirit's ministry in Ezekiel.

THE SPIRIT...

Demonstrates God's energizing power.
EZK 1:12, 20–21; 10:17

Fills people, equipping them to speak God's words.
EZK 2:2–4; 3:24–27; 11:5; 37:9–10

Leads and guides people to help them fulfill God's mission.
EZK 3:12, 14; 8:3; 11:1, 24; 37:1; 43:5

Brings new life and transformation.
EZK 11:19; 18:31; 36:26–27; 37:5–6, 14; 39:29

whose ordinances you have not practiced. Instead, you have acted according to the ordinances of the nations around you.'"

¹³ Now while I was prophesying, Pelatiah son of Benaiah died. Then I fell facedown and cried out loudly, "Oh, Lord GOD! You are bringing the remnant of Israel to an end!"

◗ GOING DEEPER

EXODUS 40:34-35
THE LORD'S GLORY

³⁴ The cloud covered the tent of meeting, and the glory of the LORD filled the tabernacle. ³⁵ Moses was unable to enter the tent of meeting because the cloud rested on it, and the glory of the LORD filled the tabernacle.

1 KINGS 8:3-11

³ All the elders of Israel came, and the priests picked up the ark. ⁴ The priests and the Levites brought the ark of the LORD, the tent of meeting, and the holy utensils that were in the tent. ⁵ King Solomon and the entire congregation of Israel, who had gathered around him and were with him in front of the ark, were sacrificing sheep, goats, and cattle that could not be counted or numbered, because there were so many. ⁶ The priests brought the ark of the LORD's covenant to its place, into the inner sanctuary of the temple, to the most holy place beneath the wings of the cherubim. ⁷ For the cherubim were spreading their wings over the place of the ark, so that the cherubim covered the ark and its poles from above. ⁸ The poles were so long that their ends were seen from the holy place in front of the inner sanctuary, but they were not seen from outside the sanctuary; they are still there today. ⁹ Nothing was in the ark except the two stone tablets that Moses had put there at Horeb, where the LORD made a covenant with the Israelites when they came out of the land of Egypt.

¹⁰ When the priests came out of the holy place, the cloud filled the LORD's temple, ¹¹ and because of the cloud, the priests were not able to continue ministering, for the glory of the LORD filled the temple.

Notes

"I will give them integrity of heart and put a new spirit within them."

EZEKIEL 11:19

The Promise of Israel's Restoration

EZEKIEL 11:14–25

PROMISE OF ISRAEL'S RESTORATION

14 The word of the LORD came to me again: 15 "Son of man, your own relatives, those who have the right to redeem your property, along with the entire house of Israel—all of them—are those to whom the residents of Jerusalem have said, 'You are far from the LORD; this land has been given to us as a possession.'

16 "Therefore say, 'This is what the Lord GOD says: Though I sent them far away among the nations and scattered them among the countries, yet for a little while I have been a sanctuary for them in the countries where they have gone.'

17 "Therefore say, 'This is what the Lord GOD says: I will gather you from the peoples and assemble you from the countries where you have been scattered, and I will give you the land of Israel.'

18 "When they arrive there, they will remove all its abhorrent acts and detestable practices from it. 19 I will give them integrity of heart and put a new spirit within them; I will remove their heart of stone from their bodies and give them a heart of flesh, 20 so that they will follow my statutes, keep my ordinances, and practice them. They will be my people, and I will be their God. 21 But as for those whose hearts pursue their desire for abhorrent acts and detestable practices, I will bring their conduct down on their own heads." This is the declaration of the Lord GOD.

GOD'S GLORY LEAVES JERUSALEM

22 Then the cherubim, with the wheels beside them, lifted their wings, and the glory of the God of Israel was above them. 23 The glory of the LORD rose up from within the city and stopped on the mountain east of the city. 24 The Spirit lifted me up and brought me to Chaldea and to the exiles in a vision from the Spirit of God. After the vision I had seen left me, 25 I spoke to the exiles about all the things the LORD had shown me.

EZEKIEL 12

EZEKIEL DRAMATIZES THE EXILE

1 The word of the LORD came to me: 2 "Son of man, you are living among a rebellious house. They have eyes to see but do not see, and ears to hear but do not hear, for they are a rebellious house.

3 "Now you, son of man, get your bags ready for exile and go into exile in their sight during the day. You will go into exile from your place to another place while they watch; perhaps

they will understand, though they are a rebellious house. ⁴ During the day, bring out your bags like an exile's bags while they look on. Then in the evening go out in their sight like those going into exile. ⁵ As they watch, dig through the wall and take the bags out through it. ⁶ And while they look on, lift the bags to your shoulder and take them out in the dark; cover your face so that you cannot see the land. For I have made you a sign to the house of Israel."

⁷ So I did just as I was commanded. In the daytime I brought out my bags like an exile's bags. In the evening I dug through the wall by hand; I took them out in the dark, carrying them on my shoulder in their sight.

⁸ In the morning the word of the LORD came to me: ⁹ "Son of man, hasn't the house of Israel, that rebellious house, asked you, 'What are you doing?' ¹⁰ Say to them, 'This is what the Lord GOD says: This pronouncement concerns the prince in Jerusalem and the whole house of Israel living there.' ¹¹ You are to say, 'I am a sign for you. Just as I have done, it will be done to them; they will go into exile, into captivity.' ¹² The prince who is among them will lift his bags to his shoulder in the dark and go out. They will dig through the wall to bring him out through it. He will cover his face so he cannot see the land with his eyes. ¹³ But I will spread my net over him, and he will be caught in my snare. I will bring him to Babylon, the land of the Chaldeans, yet he will not see it, and he will die there. ¹⁴ I will also scatter all the attendants who surround him and all his troops to every direction of the wind, and I will draw a sword to chase after them. ¹⁵ They will know that I am the LORD when I disperse them among the nations and scatter them among the countries. ¹⁶ But I will spare a few of them from the sword, famine, and plague, so that among the nations where they go they can tell about all their detestable practices. Then they will know that I am the LORD."

EZEKIEL DRAMATIZES ISRAEL'S ANXIETY

¹⁷ The word of the LORD came to me: ¹⁸ "Son of man, eat your bread with trembling and drink your water with anxious shaking. ¹⁹ Then say to the people of the land, 'This is what the Lord GOD says about the residents of Jerusalem in the land of Israel: They will eat their bread with anxiety and drink their water in dread, for their land will be stripped of everything in it because of the violence of all who live there. ²⁰ The inhabited cities will be destroyed, and the land will become dreadful. Then you will know that I am the LORD.'"

A DECEPTIVE PROVERB STOPPED

²¹ Again the word of the LORD came to me: ²² "Son of man, what is this proverb you people have about the land of Israel, which goes, 'The days keep passing by, and every vision fails'? ²³ Therefore say to them, 'This is what the Lord GOD says: I will put a stop to this proverb, and they will not use it again in Israel.' But say to them, 'The days have arrived, as well as the fulfillment of every vision. ²⁴ For there will no longer be any false vision or flattering divination within the house of Israel.

²⁵ But I, the LORD, will speak whatever message I will speak, and it will be done. It will no longer be delayed. For in your days, rebellious house, I will speak a message and bring it to pass. This is the declaration of the Lord GOD.'"

²⁶ The word of the LORD came to me: ²⁷ "Son of man, notice that the house of Israel is saying, 'The vision that he sees concerns many years from now; he prophesies about distant times.' ²⁸ Therefore say to them, 'This is what the Lord GOD says: None of my words will be delayed any longer. The message I speak will be fulfilled. This is the declaration of the Lord GOD.'"

◤ GOING DEEPER

PSALM 2:1-6

CORONATION OF THE SON

¹ Why do the nations rage
and the peoples plot in vain?
² The kings of the earth take their stand,
and the rulers conspire together
against the LORD and his Anointed One:
³ "Let's tear off their chains
and throw their ropes off of us."

⁴ The one enthroned in heaven laughs;
the Lord ridicules them.
⁵ Then he speaks to them in his anger
and terrifies them in his wrath:

⁶ "I HAVE INSTALLED MY KING
ON ZION, MY HOLY MOUNTAIN."

MATTHEW 13:16-17

¹⁶ "Blessed are your eyes because they do see, and your ears because they do hear. ¹⁷ For truly I tell you, many prophets and righteous people longed to see the things you see but didn't see them, to hear the things you hear but didn't hear them."

Notes

God preserves His own: Those who have not turned away to idols

The Promise of Restoration in Ezekiel's Visions

Ezekiel's visions were central to his ministry as a prophet. God gave Ezekiel insight into the destruction that would come to the city of Jerusalem because of the Israelites' idolatrous hearts. These visions also foretold the ultimate restoration of all creation through God's redeeming grace. The list below gives an overview of Ezekiel's different visions and their meanings.

EZEKIEL'S VISION

THE LORD'S GLORY

Four living creatures with four wheels (Ezk 1:4–21)

A glimmering presence spread out above the four creatures (Ezk 1:22–24)

A human-like form on a throne, surrounded by brilliant light (Ezk 1:25–28)

THE FALL OF JERUSALEM

Wickedness in the temple (Ezk 8:5–18)

The slaughter of the inhabitants of Jerusalem (Ezk 9)

God's presence and glory depart from the temple in Jerusalem (Ezk 10)

Corrupt leaders in Jerusalem and the Lord's presence leaving the city (Ezk 11)

MEANING

The bright light and the chariot represented the presence of God, which had been in the temple in Jerusalem but was now appearing to Ezekiel in Babylon.

The glory of the Lord spoke from the chariot, calling Ezekiel to prophesy the judgment on Jerusalem because of Israel's idolatry. Despite the impending judgment, the rainbow in the vision served as a reminder of the covenant God had made in the days of Noah to never again fully destroy humanity. This symbol served as a reminder of God's coming restoration.

Then he said to me: "Son of man, go to the house of Israel and speak my words to them…But the house of Israel will not want to listen to you because they do not want to listen to me."

EZK 3:4, 7

This unfolding scene of the priests and worshipers abandoning God to worship idols is the reason why the Lord's presence appeared to Ezekiel in Babylon. The presence of the Lord left the temple and the city of Jerusalem, but He still promised to restore His people and His presence.

"I will give them integrity of heart and put a new spirit within them; I will remove their heart of stone from their bodies and give them a heart of flesh, so that they will follow my statutes, keep my ordinances, and practice them. They will be my people, and I will be their God."

EZK 11:19–20

THE VALLEY OF DRY BONES

A valley of dry human bones, which the Lord commands Ezekiel to speak His word over (Ezk 37:1–6)

The bones rattle and assemble into skeletons, covered with flesh, after Ezekiel does as the Lord commanded him (Ezk 37:7–10)

The bones fill with breath and stand on their feet as a vast army of living people (Ezk 37:10)

THE NEW TEMPLE AND THE NEW CITY

The outer and inner courts of a new temple (Ezk 40)

The temple itself, with its inner chambers (Ezk 41–42)

The return of the Lord's glory (Ezk 43:1–12)

New worship in the new temple, complete with priests, offerings, and an altar (Ezk 44–46)

A new holy land, with a river of life running through it, secure and defined boundaries, and a new holy city (Ezk 47–48)

The bones represented the kingdoms of Israel and Judah in their current state—divided, dead, dry, and ruined. But God brought what was dead back to life, a reminder of His promise to unify and restore Israel by pouring out His Spirit upon them and giving them hearts of flesh instead of their hearts of stone.

"These bones are the whole house of Israel…'I will put my Spirit in you, and you will live, and I will settle you in your own land. Then you will know that I am the LORD.'"

EZK 37:11, 14

After Israel's rebellion against God, the destruction of Jerusalem and the departure of the Lord's presence, the Lord promised that by His Spirit, He will bring the dead back to life and restore the ruins of Jerusalem into a glorious new city. There, the presence of the Lord will return to dwell among His people in a city that will never fall.

I saw the glory of the God of Israel coming from the east. His voice sounded like the roar of a huge torrent, and the earth shone with his glory…The glory of the LORD entered the temple by way of the gate that faced east. Then the Spirit lifted me up and brought me to the inner court, and the glory of the LORD filled the temple.

EZK 43:2, 4–5

"The perimeter of the city will be six miles, and the name of the city from that day on will be, The LORD Is There."

EZK 48:35

Israel's False Prophets Condemned

11

EZEKIEL 13

ISRAEL'S FALSE PROPHETS CONDEMNED

¹ The word of the LORD came to me: ² "Son of man, prophesy against the prophets of Israel who are prophesying. Say to those who prophesy out of their own imagination, 'Hear the word of the LORD! ³ This is what the Lord GOD says: Woe to the foolish prophets who follow their own spirit and have seen nothing. ⁴ Your prophets, Israel, are like jackals among ruins. ⁵ You did not go up to the gaps or restore the wall around the house of Israel so that it might stand in battle on the day of the LORD. ⁶ They saw false visions and their divinations were a lie. They claimed, "This is the LORD's declaration," when the LORD did not send them, yet they wait for the fulfillment of their message. ⁷ Didn't you see a false vision and speak a lying divination when you proclaimed, "This is the LORD's declaration," even though I had not spoken?

⁸ "'Therefore, this is what the Lord GOD says: You have spoken falsely and had lying visions; that's why you discover that I am against you. This is the declaration of the Lord GOD. ⁹ My hand will be against the prophets who see false visions and speak lying divinations. They will not be present in the council of my people or be recorded in the register of the house of Israel, and they will not enter the land of Israel. Then you will know that I am the Lord GOD.

¹⁰ "'Since they have led my people astray by saying, "Peace," when there is no peace, and since when a flimsy wall is being built, they plaster it with whitewash, ¹¹ therefore, tell those plastering it with whitewash that it will fall. Torrential rain will come, and I will send hailstones plunging down, and a whirlwind will be released. ¹² When the wall has fallen, will you not be asked, "Where's the whitewash you plastered on it?"

¹³ "'So this is what the Lord GOD says: I will release a whirlwind in my wrath. Torrential rain will come in my anger, and hailstones will fall in destructive fury. ¹⁴ I will demolish the wall you plastered with whitewash and knock it to the ground so that its foundation is exposed. The city will fall, and you will be destroyed within it. Then you will know that I am the LORD. ¹⁵ After I exhaust my wrath against the wall and against those who plaster it with whitewash, I will say to you, "The wall is no more and neither are those who plastered it— ¹⁶ those prophets of Israel who prophesied to Jerusalem and saw a vision of peace for her when there was no peace." This is the declaration of the Lord GOD.'

¹⁷ "Now you, son of man, face the women among your people who prophesy out of their own imagination, and prophesy against them. ¹⁸ Say, 'This is what the Lord GOD says: Woe to the women who sew magic bands on the wrist of every hand and who make veils for the heads of people of every size in order to ensnare lives. Will you ensnare the lives of my people but preserve your own? ¹⁹ You profane me among my people for handfuls of barley and scraps of bread; you put those to death who should not die and spare those who should not live, when you lie to my people, who listen to lies.

²⁰ "'Therefore, this is what the Lord GOD says: I am against your magic bands with which you ensnare people like birds, and I will tear them from your arms. I will free the people you have ensnared like birds. ²¹ I will also tear off your veils and rescue my people from your hands, so that they will no longer be prey in your hands. Then you will know that I am the LORD. ²² Because you have disheartened the righteous person with lies (when I intended no distress), and because you have supported the wicked person so that he does not turn from his evil way to save his life, ²³ therefore you will no longer see false visions or practice divination. I will rescue my people from your hands. Then you will know that I am the LORD.'"

EZEKIEL 14

IDOLATROUS ELDERS PUNISHED

¹ Some of the elders of Israel came to me and sat down in front of me. ² Then the word of the LORD came to me: ³ "Son of man, these men have set up idols in their hearts and have put their sinful stumbling blocks in front of themselves. Should I actually let them inquire of me?

⁴ "Therefore, speak to them and tell them, 'This is what the Lord GOD says: When anyone from the house of Israel sets up idols in his heart and puts his sinful stumbling block in

front of himself, and then comes to the prophet, I, the LORD, will answer him appropriately. I will answer him according to his many idols, [5] so that I may take hold of the house of Israel by their hearts. They are all estranged from me because of their idols.'

[6] "Therefore, say to the house of Israel, 'This is what the Lord GOD says: Repent and turn away from your idols; turn your faces away from all your detestable things. [7] For when anyone from the house of Israel or from the aliens who reside in Israel separates himself from me, setting up idols in his heart and putting his sinful stumbling block in front of himself, and then comes to the prophet to inquire of me, I, the LORD, will answer him myself. [8] I will turn against that one and make him a sign and a proverb; I will cut him off from among my people. Then you will know that I am the LORD.

[9] "'But if the prophet is deceived and speaks a message, it was I, the LORD, who deceived that prophet. I will stretch out my hand against him and destroy him from among my people Israel. [10] They will bear their punishment—the punishment of the one who inquires will be the same as that of the prophet— [11] in order that the house of Israel may no longer stray from following me and no longer defile themselves with all their transgressions. Then they will be my people and I will be their God. This is the declaration of the Lord GOD.'"

FOUR DEVASTATING JUDGMENTS

[12] The word of the LORD came to me: [13] "Son of man, suppose a land sins against me by acting faithlessly, and I stretch out my hand against it to cut off its supply of bread, to send famine through it, and to wipe out both people and animals from it. [14] Even if these three men—Noah, Daniel, and Job—were in it, they would rescue only themselves by their righteousness." This is the declaration of the Lord GOD.

[15] "Suppose I allow dangerous animals to pass through the land and depopulate it so that it becomes desolate, with no one passing through it for fear of the animals. [16] Even if these three men were in it, as I live"—the declaration of the Lord GOD— "they could not rescue their sons or daughters. They alone would be rescued, but the land would be desolate.

[17] "Or suppose I bring a sword against that land and say, 'Let a sword pass through it,' so that I wipe out both people and animals from it. [18] Even if these three men were in it, as I live"—the declaration of the Lord GOD—"they could not rescue their sons or daughters, but they alone would be rescued.

[19] "Or suppose I send a plague into that land and pour out my wrath on it with bloodshed to wipe out both people and animals from it. [20] Even if Noah, Daniel, and Job were in it, as I live"—the declaration of the Lord GOD—"they could not rescue their son or daughter. They would rescue only themselves by their righteousness.

21 "For this is what the Lord God says: How much worse will it be when I send my four devastating judgments against Jerusalem—sword, famine, dangerous animals, and plague—in order to wipe out both people and animals from it! 22 Even so, there will be survivors left in it, sons and daughters who will be brought out. Indeed, they will come out to you, and you will observe their conduct and actions. Then you will be consoled about the devastation I have brought on Jerusalem, about all I have brought on it. 23 They will bring you consolation when you see their conduct and actions, and you will know that it was not without cause that I have done what I did to it." This is the declaration of the Lord God.

🛡 GOING DEEPER

ISAIAH 55:8-11

8 "For my thoughts are not your thoughts,
and your ways are not my ways."
    This is the Lord's declaration.
9 "For as heaven is higher than earth,
so my ways are higher than your ways,
and my thoughts than your thoughts.
10 For just as rain and snow fall from heaven
and do not return there
without saturating the earth
and making it germinate and sprout,
and providing seed to sow
and food to eat,
11 so my word that comes from my mouth
will not return to me empty,
but it will accomplish what I please
and will prosper in what I send it to do."

A Parable of Jerusalem's Unfaithfulness

DAY 12

EZEKIEL 15
PARABLE OF THE USELESS VINE

[1] Then the word of the LORD came to me: [2] "Son of man, how does the wood of the vine, that branch among the trees of the forest, compare to any other wood? [3] Can wood be taken from it to make something useful? Or can anyone make a peg from it to hang things on? [4] In fact, it is put into the fire as fuel. The fire devours both of its ends, and the middle is charred. Can it be useful for anything? [5] Even when it was whole it could not be made into a useful object. How much less can it ever be made into anything useful when the fire has devoured it and it is charred!"

[6] Therefore, this is what the Lord GOD says, "Like the wood of the vine among the trees of the forest, which I have given to the fire as fuel, so I will give up the residents of Jerusalem. [7] I will turn against them. They may have escaped from the fire, but it will still consume them. And you will know that I am the LORD when I turn against them. [8] I will make the land desolate because they have acted unfaithfully." This is the declaration of the Lord GOD.

EZEKIEL 16
PARABLE OF GOD'S ADULTEROUS WIFE

[1] The word of the LORD came to me again: [2] "Son of man, confront Jerusalem with her detestable practices. [3] You are to say, 'This is what the Lord GOD says to Jerusalem: Your origin and your birth were in the land of the Canaanites. Your father was an Amorite and your mother a Hethite. [4] As for your birth, your umbilical cord wasn't cut on the day you were born, and you weren't washed clean with water. You were not rubbed with salt or wrapped in cloths. [5] No one cared enough about you to do even one of these things out of compassion for you. But you were thrown out into the open field because you were despised on the day you were born.

[6] "'I passed by you and saw you thrashing around in your blood, and I said to you as you lay in your blood, "Live!" Yes, I said to you as you lay in your blood, "Live!" [7] I made you thrive like plants of the field. You grew up and matured and became very beautiful. Your breasts were formed and your hair grew, but you were stark naked.

8 "'Then I passed by you and saw you, and you were indeed at the age for love. So I spread the edge of my garment over you and covered your nakedness. I pledged myself to you, entered into a covenant with you—this is the declaration of the Lord God—and you became mine. 9 I washed you with water, rinsed off your blood, and anointed you with oil. 10 I clothed you in embroidered cloth and provided you with fine leather sandals. I also wrapped you in fine linen and covered you with silk. 11 I adorned you with jewelry, putting bracelets on your wrists and a necklace around your neck. 12 I put a ring in your nose, earrings on your ears, and a beautiful crown on your head. 13 So you were adorned with gold and silver, and your clothing was made of fine linen, silk, and embroidered cloth. You ate fine flour, honey, and oil. You became extremely beautiful and attained royalty. 14 Your fame spread among the nations because of your beauty, for it was perfect through my splendor, which I had bestowed on you. This is the declaration of the Lord God.

15 "'But you trusted in your beauty and acted like a prostitute because of your fame. You lavished your sexual favors on everyone who passed by. Your beauty became his. 16 You took some of your clothing and made colorful high places for yourself, and you engaged in prostitution on them. These places should not have been built, and this should never have happened! 17 You also took your beautiful jewelry made from the gold and silver I had given you, and you made male images so that you could engage in prostitution with them. 18 Then you took your embroidered clothing to cover them and set my oil and incense before them. 19 The food that I gave you—the fine flour, oil, and honey that I fed you—you set it before them as a pleasing aroma. That is what happened. This is the declaration of the Lord God.

20 "'You even took your sons and daughters you bore to me and sacrificed them to these images as food. Wasn't your prostitution enough? 21 You slaughtered my children and gave them up when you passed them through the fire to the images. 22 In all your detestable practices and acts of prostitution, you did not remember the days of your youth when you were stark naked and thrashing around in your blood.

23 "'Then after all your evil—Woe, woe to you!—the declaration of the Lord God— 24 you built yourself a mound and made yourself an elevated place in every square. 25 You built your elevated place at the head of every street and turned your beauty into a detestable thing. You spread your legs to everyone who passed by and increased your prostitution. 26 You engaged in promiscuous acts with Egyptian men, your well-endowed neighbors, and increased your prostitution to anger me.

27 "'Therefore, I stretched out my hand against you and reduced your provisions. I gave you over to the desire of those who hate you, the Philistine women, who were embarrassed by your indecent conduct. 28 Then you engaged in prostitution with the Assyrian men because you were not satisfied. Even though you did this with them, you were still not satisfied. 29 So you extended your prostitution to Chaldea, the land of merchants, but you were not even satisfied with this!

30 "'How your heart was inflamed with lust—the declaration of the Lord God—when you did all these things, the acts of a brazen prostitute, 31 building your mound at the head of every street and making your elevated place in every square. But you were unlike a prostitute because you scorned payment. 32 You adulterous wife, who receives strangers instead of her husband! 33 Men give gifts to all prostitutes, but you gave gifts to all your lovers. You bribed them to come to you from all around for your sexual favors. 34 So you were the opposite of other women in your acts of prostitution; no one solicited you. When you paid a fee instead of one being paid to you, you were the opposite.

35 "'Therefore, you prostitute, hear the word of the Lord! 36 This is what the Lord God says: Because your lust was poured out and your nakedness exposed by your acts of prostitution with your lovers, and because of all your detestable idols and the blood of your children that you gave to them, 37 I am therefore going to gather all the lovers you pleased—all those you loved as well as all those you hated. I will gather them against you from all around and expose your nakedness to them so they see you completely naked. 38 I will judge you the way adulteresses and those who shed blood are judged. Then I will bring about the shedding of your blood in jealous wrath. 39 I will hand you over to them, and they will demolish your mounds and tear down your

elevated places. They will strip off your clothes, take your beautiful jewelry, and leave you stark naked. [40] They will bring a mob against you to stone you and to cut you to pieces with their swords. [41] They will burn your houses and execute judgments against you in the sight of many women. I will stop you from being a prostitute, and you will never again pay fees for lovers. [42] So I will satisfy my wrath against you, and my jealousy will turn away from you. Then I will be calm and no longer angry. [43] Because you did not remember the days of your youth but enraged me with all these things, I will also bring your conduct down on your own head. This is the declaration of the Lord God. Haven't you committed depravity in addition to all your detestable practices?

[44] "'Look, everyone who uses proverbs will quote this proverb about you: "Like mother, like daughter." [45] You are the daughter of your mother, who despised her husband and children. You are the sister of your sisters, who despised their husbands and children. Your mother was a Hethite and your father an Amorite. [46] Your older sister was Samaria, who lived with her daughters to the north of you, and your younger sister was Sodom, who lived with her daughters to the south of you. [47] Didn't you walk in their ways and do their detestable practices? It was only a short time before all your ways were more corrupt than theirs.

[48] "'As I live—the declaration of the Lord God—your sister Sodom and her daughters have not behaved as you and your daughters have. [49] Now this was the iniquity of your sister Sodom: She and her daughters had pride, plenty of food, and comfortable security, but didn't support the poor and needy. [50] They were haughty and did detestable acts before me, so I removed them when I saw this. [51] But Samaria did not commit even half your sins. You have multiplied your detestable practices beyond theirs and made your sisters appear righteous by all the detestable acts you have committed. [52] You must also bear your disgrace, since you have helped your sisters out. For they appear more righteous than you because of your sins, which you committed more detestably than they did. So you also, be ashamed and bear your disgrace, since you have made your sisters appear righteous.

[53] "'I will restore their fortunes, the fortunes of Sodom and her daughters and those of Samaria and her daughters. I will also restore your fortunes among them, [54] so you will bear your disgrace and be ashamed of all you did when you comforted them. [55] As for your sisters, Sodom and her daughters and Samaria and her daughters will return to their former state. You and your daughters will also return to your former state. [56] Didn't you treat your sister Sodom as an object of scorn when you were proud, [57] before your wickedness was exposed? It was like the time you were scorned by the daughters of Aram and all those around her, and by the daughters of the Philistines—those who treated you with contempt from every side. [58] You yourself must bear the consequences of your depravity and detestable practices—this is the Lord's declaration.

⁵⁹ "'For this is what the Lord God says: I will deal with you according to what you have done, since you have despised the oath by breaking the covenant.

⁶⁰ BUT I WILL REMEMBER THE COVENANT I MADE WITH YOU IN THE DAYS OF YOUR YOUTH, AND I WILL ESTABLISH A PERMANENT COVENANT WITH YOU.

⁶¹ Then you will remember your ways and be ashamed when you receive your older and younger sisters. I will give them to you as daughters, but not because of your covenant. ⁶² I will establish my covenant with you, and you will know that I am the Lord, ⁶³ so that when I make atonement for all you have done, you will remember and be ashamed, and never open your mouth again because of your disgrace. This is the declaration of the Lord God.'"

◆ GOING DEEPER

ECCLESIASTES 12:1

So remember your Creator in the days of your youth:

> Before the days of adversity come,
> and the years approach when you will say,
> "I have no delight in them"…

JOHN 15:1-5

THE VINE AND THE BRANCHES

¹ "I am the true vine, and my Father is the gardener. ² Every branch in me that does not produce fruit he removes, and he prunes every branch that produces fruit so that it will produce more fruit. ³ You are already clean because of the word I have spoken to you. ⁴ Remain in me, and I in you. Just as a branch is unable to produce fruit by itself unless it remains on the vine, neither can you unless you remain in me. ⁵ I am the vine; you are the branches. The one who remains in me and I in him produces much fruit, because you can do nothing without me."

Response

LAMENT

During this Lenten season, we make time to lament— to grieve our own sin and express sorrow over the brokenness of the world, to which our sin contributes.

1 What in your life do you need to lament? Take time to confess your own sin and grieve over how the sin of others has affected you.

2 How does your sin and brokenness affect your community? Take time to lament for the brokenness you see in the world.

CONFESSION AND ASSURANCE

A lament is not a quick
fix, but God is faithful,
and lamenting gently but
persistently reminds us to
trust Him. Use this space to
confess your need for God
and His intervention, as well
as express your continued
hope found in His provision.

Asparagus Prosciutto Tart

SERVES 8

INGREDIENTS

CRUST

3 cups blanched almond flour

1 egg

¼ cup arrowroot powder

2 tablespoons melted coconut oil

2 tablespoons cold water

½ teaspoon fine sea salt

FILLING

3 tablespoons extra-virgin olive oil

1 pound asparagus, trimmed and cut diagonally into ½-inch pieces

Juice from 1 lemon

2 cloves garlic, minced

⅓ cup cashew cream

6 eggs

½ teaspoon fine sea salt

¼ teaspoon freshly ground black pepper

6 ounces thinly sliced prosciutto, cut into ribbons

1 cup microgreens

3 tablespoons chopped fresh chives

DIRECTIONS

Preheat the oven to 325°F. Lightly grease an 11 by 7-inch tart pan.

To make the crust, combine the almond flour, egg, arrowroot, coconut oil, water, and salt in a stand mixer fitted with the beater attachment, or use an electric handheld mixer. Beat on medium speed until a loose dough forms. Gather the dough and press it into the bottom and up the sides of the tart pan. Bake for 15 minutes, or until the crust is golden on the edges. Remove the crust from the oven and increase the temperature to 375°F.

To make the filling, heat 1 tablespoon of the olive oil in a skillet over medium-high heat. Add the asparagus and ½ teaspoon of the lemon juice and saute for 3 minutes. Add the garlic and continue cooking for 2 minutes, or until the asparagus is crisp-tender.

Spread the cashew cream on the bottom of the crust, then spoon in the asparagus mixture. Gently crack the eggs on top, spacing them out evenly. Sprinkle with the salt and pepper. Bake for 10 to 12 minutes, just until the egg whites are set and the yolks are still soft.

Remove from the oven and sprinkle with the prosciutto, microgreens, and chives. Drizzle with the remaining 2 tablespoons olive oil and the remaining lemon juice. Serve immediately.

Rebecca Hunter, *Leaves the 99*, 2018, oil on canvas, 36x60 in.

GRACE DAY

"You are already clean because
of the word I have spoken to you."

JOHN 15:3

DAY 13

Lent is a season where we reflect on the depth of our sin and embrace the hope and strength found only in the cross of Christ. We seek unhurried moments of quiet to read Scripture, pray, confess, and repent. Take some time today to catch up on your reading, make space for prayer, and rest in God's presence.

14

Weekly Truth

Scripture is God-breathed and true. When we memorize it, we carry His Word with us wherever we go.

This week we will continue to memorize Ezekiel 36:26–28 by adding the second half of verse 26, where God promises to remove Israel's heart of stone. Jesus fulfilled this promise for us with His death on the cross.

"I will give you a new heart and put a new spirit within you; **I will remove your heart of stone and give you a heart of flesh.** I will place my Spirit within you and cause you to follow my statutes and carefully observe my ordinances. You will live in the land that I gave your ancestors; you will be my people, and I will be your God."

EZEKIEL 36:26–28

See tips for memorizing Scripture on page 236.

"This vine bent its roots toward him! It stretched out its branches to him."

EZEKIEL 17:7

The Parable of the Eagles

EZEKIEL 17

THE PARABLE OF THE EAGLES

¹ The word of the LORD came to me: ² "Son of man, pose a riddle and speak a parable to the house of Israel. ³ You are to say, 'This is what the Lord GOD says: A huge eagle with powerful wings, long feathers, and full plumage of many colors came to Lebanon and took the top of the cedar. ⁴ He plucked off its topmost shoot, brought it to the land of merchants, and set it in a city of traders. ⁵ Then he took some of the land's seed and put it in a fertile field; he set it like a willow, a plant by abundant water. ⁶ It sprouted and became a spreading vine, low in height with its branches turned toward him, yet its roots stayed under it. So it became a vine, produced branches, and sent out shoots.

⁷ "'But there was another huge eagle with powerful wings and thick plumage. And this vine bent its roots toward him! It stretched out its branches to him from the plot where it was planted, so that he might water it. ⁸ It had been planted in a good field by abundant water in order to produce branches, bear fruit, and become a splendid vine.'

⁹ "You are to say, 'This is what the Lord GOD says: Will it flourish? Will he not tear out its roots and strip off its fruit so that it shrivels? All its fresh leaves will wither! Great strength and many people will not be needed to pull it from its roots. ¹⁰ Even though it is planted, will it flourish? Won't it wither completely when the east wind strikes it? It will wither on the plot where it sprouted.'"

¹¹ The word of the LORD came to me: ¹² "Now say to that rebellious house, 'Don't you know what these things mean?' Tell them, 'The king of Babylon came to Jerusalem, took its king and officials, and brought them back with him to Babylon. ¹³ He took one of the royal family and made a covenant with him, putting him under oath. Then he took away the leading men of the land, ¹⁴ so that the kingdom would be humble and not exalt itself but would keep his covenant in order to endure. ¹⁵ However, this king revolted against him by sending his ambassadors to Egypt so they might give him horses and a large army. Will he flourish? Will the one who does such things escape? Can he break a covenant and still escape?

¹⁶ "'As I live—this is the declaration of the Lord GOD—he will die in Babylon, in the land of the king who put him on the throne, whose oath he despised and whose covenant he broke. ¹⁷ Pharaoh with his mighty army and vast company will not help him in battle, when ramps are built and siege walls constructed to destroy many lives. ¹⁸ He despised the oath by breaking the covenant. He did all these things even though he gave his hand in pledge. He will not escape!

[19] "'Therefore, this is what the Lord GOD says: As I live, I will bring down on his head my oath that he despised and my covenant that he broke. [20] I will spread my net over him, and he will be caught in my snare. I will bring him to Babylon and execute judgment on him there for the treachery he committed against me. [21] All the fugitives among his troops will fall by the sword, and those who survive will be scattered to every direction of the wind. Then you will know that I, the LORD, have spoken.

[22] "'This is what the Lord GOD says:

I will take a sprig
from the lofty top of the cedar and plant it.
I will pluck a tender sprig
from its topmost shoots,
and I will plant it
on a high towering mountain.
[23] I will plant it on Israel's high mountain
so that it may bear branches, produce fruit,
and become a majestic cedar.
Birds of every kind will nest under it,
taking shelter in the shade of its branches.
[24] Then all the trees of the field will know
that I am the LORD.
I bring down the tall tree,
and make the low tree tall.
I cause the green tree to wither
and make the withered tree thrive.
I, the LORD, have spoken
and I will do it.'"

🦋 GOING DEEPER

MATTHEW 11:20–30

[20] Then he proceeded to denounce the towns where most of his miracles were done, because they did not repent: [21] "Woe to you, Chorazin! Woe to you, Bethsaida! For if the miracles that were done in you had been done in Tyre and Sidon, they would have repented in sackcloth and ashes long ago. [22] But I tell you, it will be more tolerable for Tyre and Sidon on the day of judgment than for you. [23] And you, Capernaum, will you be exalted to heaven? No, you will go down to Hades. For if the miracles that were done in you had been done in Sodom, it would have remained until today. [24] But I tell you, it will be more tolerable for the land of Sodom on the day of judgment than for you."

THE SON GIVES KNOWLEDGE AND REST

[25] At that time Jesus said, "I praise you, Father, Lord of heaven and earth, because you have hidden these things from the wise and intelligent and revealed them to infants. [26] Yes, Father, because this was your good pleasure.

[27] ALL THINGS HAVE BEEN ENTRUSTED TO ME BY MY FATHER. NO ONE KNOWS THE SON EXCEPT THE FATHER, AND NO ONE KNOWS THE FATHER EXCEPT THE SON AND ANYONE TO WHOM THE SON DESIRES TO REVEAL HIM.

[28] "Come to me, all of you who are weary and burdened, and I will give you rest. [29] Take up my yoke and learn from me, because I am lowly and humble in heart, and you will find rest for your souls. [30] For my yoke is easy and my burden is light."

MATTHEW 13:24–30

THE PARABLE OF THE WHEAT AND THE WEEDS

[24] He presented another parable to them: "The kingdom of heaven may be compared to a man who sowed good seed in his field. [25] But while people were sleeping, his enemy came, sowed weeds among the wheat, and left. [26] When the plants sprouted and produced grain, then the weeds also appeared. [27] The landowner's servants came to him and said, 'Master, didn't you sow good seed in your field? Then where did the weeds come from?'

[28] "'An enemy did this,' he told them.

"'So, do you want us to go and pull them up?' the servants asked him.

[29] "'No,' he said. 'When you pull up the weeds, you might also uproot the wheat with them. [30] Let both grow together until the harvest. At harvest time I'll tell the reapers: Gather the weeds first and tie them in bundles to burn them, but collect the wheat in my barn.'"

Notes

A Personal Responsibility for Sin

EZEKIEL 18

A PERSONAL RESPONSIBILITY FOR SIN

¹ The word of the LORD came to me: ² "What do you mean by using this proverb concerning the land of Israel:

'The fathers eat sour grapes,
and the children's teeth are set on edge'?

³ As I live"—this is the declaration of the Lord GOD—"you will no longer use this proverb in Israel. ⁴ Look, every life belongs to me. The life of the father is like the life of the son—both belong to me. The person who sins is the one who will die.

⁵ "Suppose a man is righteous and does what is just and right: ⁶ He does not eat at the mountain shrines or look to the idols of the house of Israel. He does not defile his neighbor's wife or approach a woman during her menstrual impurity. ⁷ He doesn't oppress anyone but returns his collateral to the debtor. He does not commit robbery, but gives his bread to the hungry and covers the naked with clothing. ⁸ He doesn't lend at interest or for profit but keeps his hand from injustice and carries out true justice between men. ⁹ He follows my statutes and keeps my ordinances, acting faithfully. Such a person is righteous; he will certainly live." This is the declaration of the Lord GOD.

¹⁰ "But suppose the man has a violent son, who sheds blood and does any of these things, ¹¹ though the father has done none of them. Indeed, when the son eats at the mountain shrines and defiles his neighbor's wife, ¹² and when he oppresses the poor and needy, commits robbery, and does not return collateral, and when he looks to the idols, commits detestable acts, ¹³ and lends at interest or for profit, will he live? He will not live! Since he has committed all these detestable acts, he will certainly die. His death will be his own fault.

¹⁴ "Now suppose he has a son who sees all the sins his father has committed, and though he sees them, he does not do likewise. ¹⁵ He does not eat at the mountain shrines or look to the idols of the house of Israel. He does not defile his neighbor's wife. ¹⁶ He doesn't oppress anyone, hold collateral, or commit robbery. He gives his bread to the hungry and covers the naked with clothing. ¹⁷ He keeps his hand from harming the poor, not taking interest or profit on a loan. He practices my ordinances and follows my statutes. Such a person will not die for his father's iniquity. He will certainly live.

¹⁸ "As for his father, he will die for his own iniquity because he practiced fraud, robbed his brother, and did among his people what was not good. ¹⁹ But you may ask, 'Why doesn't

the son suffer punishment for the father's iniquity?' Since the son has done what is just and right, carefully observing all my statutes, he will certainly live. [20] The person who sins is the one who will die. A son won't suffer punishment for the father's iniquity, and a father won't suffer punishment for the son's iniquity. The righteousness of the righteous person will be on him, and the wickedness of the wicked person will be on him.

[21] "But if the wicked person turns from all the sins he has committed, keeps all my statutes, and does what is just and right, he will certainly live; he will not die. [22] None of the transgressions he has committed will be held against him. He will live because of the righteousness he has practiced. [23] Do I take any pleasure in the death of the wicked?" This is the declaration of the Lord God. "Instead, don't I take pleasure when he turns from his ways and lives? [24] But when a righteous person turns from his righteousness and acts unjustly, committing the same detestable acts that the wicked do, will he live? None of the righteous acts he did will be remembered. He will die because of the treachery he has engaged in and the sin he has committed.

[25] "But you say, 'The Lord's way isn't fair.' Now listen, house of Israel: Is it my way that is unfair? Instead, isn't it your ways that are unfair? [26] When a righteous person turns from his righteousness and acts unjustly, he will die for this. He will die because of the injustice he has committed. [27] But if a wicked person turns from the wickedness he has committed and does what is just and right, he will preserve his life. [28] He will certainly live because he thought it over and turned from all the transgressions he had committed; he will not die. [29] But the house of Israel says, 'The Lord's way isn't fair.'

IS IT MY WAYS THAT ARE UNFAIR, HOUSE OF ISRAEL? INSTEAD, ISN'T IT YOUR WAYS THAT ARE UNFAIR?

[30] "Therefore, house of Israel, I will judge each one of you according to his ways." This is the declaration of the Lord God. "Repent and turn from all your rebellious acts, so they will not become a sinful stumbling block to you. [31] Throw off all the transgressions you have committed, and get yourselves a new heart and a new spirit. Why should you die, house of Israel? [32] For I take no pleasure in anyone's death." This is the declaration of the Lord God. "So repent and live!"

EZEKIEL 19

A LAMENT FOR ISRAEL'S PRINCES

[1] "As for you, take up a lament for the princes of Israel, [2] and say:

What was your mother? A lioness!
She lay down among the lions;

she reared her cubs among the young lions.
³ She brought up one of her cubs,
and he became a young lion.
After he learned to tear prey,
he devoured people.
⁴ When the nations heard about him,
he was caught in their pit.
Then they led him away with hooks
to the land of Egypt.

⁵ When she saw that she waited in vain,
that her hope was lost,
she took another of her cubs
and made him a young lion.
⁶ He prowled among the lions,
and he became a young lion.
After he learned to tear prey,
he devoured people.
⁷ He devastated their strongholds
and destroyed their cities.
The land and everything in it shuddered
at the sound of his roaring.
⁸ Then the nations from the surrounding provinces
set out against him.
They spread their net over him;
he was caught in their pit.
⁹ They put a wooden yoke on him with hooks
and led him away to the king of Babylon.
They brought him into the fortresses
so his roar could no longer be heard
on the mountains of Israel.

¹⁰ Your mother was like a vine in your vineyard,
planted by the water;
it was fruitful and full of branches
because of abundant water.
¹¹ It had strong branches, fit for the scepters of rulers;
its height towered among the clouds.
So it was conspicuous for its height
as well as its many branches.
¹² But it was uprooted in fury,
thrown to the ground,
and the east wind dried up its fruit.

Its strong branches were torn off and dried up;
fire consumed them.
¹³ Now it is planted in the wilderness,
in a dry and thirsty land.
¹⁴ Fire has gone out from its main branch
and has devoured its fruit,
so that it no longer has a strong branch,
a scepter for ruling.

This is a lament and should be used as a lament."

🔖 GOING DEEPER

ROMANS 1:16–17

THE RIGHTEOUS WILL LIVE BY FAITH

¹⁶ For I am not ashamed of the gospel, because it is the power of God for salvation to everyone who believes, first to the Jew, and also to the Greek. ¹⁷ For in it the righteousness of God is revealed from faith to faith, just as it is written: The righteous will live by faith.

2 PETER 3:9

The Lord does not delay his promise, as some understand delay, but is patient with you, not wanting any to perish but all to come to repentance.

Notes

DAY 16

"I pledged myself to you, entered into a

of the Lord GOD—

covenant with you — this is the declaration and you became mine." **EZEKIEL 16:8**

Israel's Rebellion

EZEKIEL 20:1-31

ISRAEL'S REBELLION

¹ In the seventh year, in the fifth month, on the tenth day of the month, some of Israel's elders came to inquire of the LORD, and they sat down in front of me. ² Then the word of the LORD came to me: ³ "Son of man, speak with the elders of Israel and tell them, 'This is what the Lord GOD says: Are you coming to inquire of me? As I live, I will not let you inquire of me. This is the declaration of the Lord GOD.'

⁴ "Will you pass judgment against them, will you pass judgment, son of man? Explain the detestable practices of their ancestors to them. ⁵ Say to them, 'This is what the Lord GOD says: On the day I chose Israel, I swore an oath to the descendants of Jacob's house and made myself known to them in the land of Egypt. I swore to them, saying, I am the LORD your God." ⁶ On that day I swore to them that I would bring them out of the land of Egypt into a land I had searched out for them, a land flowing with milk and honey, the most beautiful of all lands. ⁷ I also said to them, "Throw away, each of you, the abhorrent things that you prize, and do not defile yourselves with the idols of Egypt. I am the LORD your God."

⁸ "'But they rebelled against me and were unwilling to listen to me. None of them threw away the abhorrent things that they prized, and they did not abandon the idols of Egypt. So I considered pouring out my wrath on them, exhausting my anger against them within the land of Egypt. ⁹ But I acted for the sake of my name, so that it would not be profaned in the eyes of the nations they were living among, in whose sight I had made myself known to Israel by bringing them out of Egypt.

¹⁰ "'So I brought them out of the land of Egypt and led them into the wilderness. ¹¹ Then I gave them my statutes and explained my ordinances to them—the person who does them will live by them. ¹² I also gave them my Sabbaths to serve as a sign between me and them, so that they would know that I am the LORD who consecrates them.

¹³ "'But the house of Israel rebelled against me in the wilderness. They did not follow my statutes and they rejected my ordinances—the person who does them will live by them. They also completely profaned my Sabbaths. So I considered pouring out my wrath on them in the wilderness to put an end to them. ¹⁴ But I acted for the sake of my name, so that it would not be profaned in the eyes of the nations in whose sight I had brought them out. ¹⁵ However, I swore to them in the wilderness that I would not bring them into the land I had given them—the most beautiful of all lands, flowing with milk and honey— ¹⁶ because they

rejected my ordinances, profaned my Sabbaths, and did not follow my statutes. For their hearts went after their idols. [17] Yet I spared them from destruction and did not bring them to an end in the wilderness.

[18] "'Then I said to their children in the wilderness, "Don't follow the statutes of your fathers, defile yourselves with their idols, or keep their ordinances. [19] I am the LORD your God. Follow my statutes, keep my ordinances, and practice them. [20] Keep my Sabbaths holy, and they will be a sign between me and you, so you may know that I am the LORD your God."

[21] "'But the children rebelled against me. They did not follow my statutes or carefully keep my ordinances—the person who does them will live by them. They also profaned my Sabbaths. So I considered pouring out my wrath on them and exhausting my anger against them in the wilderness.

[22] BUT I WITHHELD MY HAND AND ACTED FOR THE SAKE OF MY NAME, SO THAT IT WOULD NOT BE PROFANED IN THE EYES OF THE NATIONS IN WHOSE SIGHT I BROUGHT THEM OUT.

[23] However, I swore to them in the wilderness that I would disperse them among the nations and scatter them among the countries. [24] For they did not practice my ordinances but rejected my statutes and profaned my Sabbaths, and their eyes were fixed on their fathers' idols. [25] I also gave them statutes that were not good and ordinances they could not live by. [26] When they sacrificed every firstborn in the fire, I defiled them through their gifts in order to devastate them so they would know that I am the LORD.'

[27] "Therefore, son of man, speak to the house of Israel, and tell them, 'This is what the Lord GOD says: In this way also your ancestors blasphemed me by committing treachery against me: [28] When I brought them into the land that I swore to give them and they saw any high hill or leafy tree, they offered their sacrifices and presented their offensive offerings there. They also sent up their pleasing aromas and poured out their drink offerings there. [29] So I asked them, "What is this high place you are going to?" And it is still called Bamah today.'

[30] "Therefore say to the house of Israel, 'This is what the Lord GOD says: Are you defiling yourselves the way your ancestors did, and prostituting yourselves with their abhorrent things? [31] When you offer your gifts, sacrificing your children in the fire, you still continue to defile yourselves with all your idols today. So should I let you inquire of me, house of Israel? As I live—this is the declaration of the Lord GOD—I will not let you inquire of me!'"

HEBREWS 3:7–12

WARNING AGAINST UNBELIEF

[7] Therefore, as the Holy Spirit says:

Today, if you hear his voice,
[8] do not harden your hearts as in the rebellion,
on the day of testing in the wilderness,
[9] where your ancestors tested me, tried me,
and saw my works [10] for forty years.
Therefore I was provoked to anger with that generation
and said, "They always go astray in their hearts,
and they have not known my ways."
[11] So I swore in my anger,
"They will not enter my rest."

[12] Watch out, brothers and sisters, so that there won't be in any of you an evil, unbelieving heart that turns away from the living God.

Israel's Restoration

DAY 18

EZEKIEL 20:32-49

ISRAEL'S RESTORATION

32 "'When you say, "Let's be like the nations, like the clans of other countries, serving wood and stone," what you have in mind will never happen. 33 As I live—the declaration of the Lord God—I will reign over you with a strong hand, an outstretched arm, and outpoured wrath. 34 I will bring you from the peoples and gather you from the countries where you were scattered, with a strong hand, an outstretched arm, and outpoured wrath. 35 I will lead you into the wilderness of the peoples and enter into judgment with you there face to face. 36 Just as I entered into judgment with your ancestors in the wilderness of the land of Egypt, so I will enter into judgment with you. This is the declaration of the Lord God. 37 I will make you pass under the rod and will bring you into the bond of the covenant. 38 I will purge you of those who rebel and transgress against me. I will bring them out of the land where they live as foreign residents, but they will not enter the land of Israel. Then you will know that I am the Lord.

39 "'As for you, house of Israel, this is what the Lord God says: Go and serve your idols, each of you. But afterward you will surely listen to me, and you will no longer defile my holy name with your gifts and idols. 40 For on my holy mountain, Israel's high mountain—the declaration of the Lord God—there the entire house of Israel, all of them, will serve me in the land. There I will accept them and will require your contributions and choicest gifts, all your holy offerings. 41 When I bring you from the peoples and gather you from the countries where you have been scattered, I will accept you as a pleasing aroma. And I will demonstrate my holiness through you in the sight of the nations. 42 When I lead you into the land of Israel, the land I swore to give your ancestors, you will know that I am the Lord. 43 There you will remember your ways and all your deeds by which you have defiled yourself, and you will loathe yourselves for all the evil things you have done. 44 You will know that I am the Lord, house of Israel, when

I HAVE DEALT WITH YOU FOR THE SAKE OF MY NAME

rather than according to your evil ways and corrupt acts. This is the declaration of the Lord God.'"

94COME TO LIFE: A LENTEN STUDY OF EZEKIEL

[45] The word of the LORD came to me: [46] "Son of man, face the south and preach against it. Prophesy against the forest land in the Negev, [47] and say to the forest there, 'Hear the word of the LORD! This is what the Lord GOD says: I am about to ignite a fire in you, and it will devour every green tree and every dry tree in you. The blazing flame will not be extinguished, and every face from the south to the north will be scorched by it. [48] Then all humanity will see that I, the LORD, have kindled it. It will not be extinguished.'"

[49] Then I said, "Oh, Lord GOD, they are saying of me, 'Isn't he just composing parables?'"

EZEKIEL 21

GOD'S SWORD OF JUDGMENT

[1] The word of the LORD came to me again: [2] "Son of man, face Jerusalem and preach against the sanctuaries. Prophesy against the land of Israel, [3] and say to it, 'This is what the LORD says: I am against you. I will draw my sword from its sheath and cut off from you both the righteous and the wicked. [4] Since I will cut off both the righteous and the wicked, my sword will therefore come out of its sheath against all humanity from the south to the north. [5] So all humanity will know that I, the LORD, have taken my sword from its sheath—it will not be sheathed again.'

[6] "But you, son of man, groan! Groan bitterly with a broken heart right before their eyes. [7] And when they ask you, 'Why are you groaning?' then say, 'Because of the news that is coming. Every heart will melt, and every hand will become weak. Every spirit will be discouraged, and all knees will run with urine. Yes, it is coming and it will happen. This is the declaration of the Lord GOD.'"

[8] The word of the LORD came to me: [9] "Son of man, prophesy, 'This is what the Lord says!' You are to proclaim,

'A sword! A sword is sharpened
and also polished.
[10] It is sharpened for slaughter,
polished to flash like lightning!
Should we rejoice?
The scepter of my son,
the sword despises every tree.
[11] The sword is given to be polished,
to be grasped in the hand.
It is sharpened, and it is polished,
to be put in the hand of the slayer.'

[12] "Cry out and wail, son of man, for it is against my people. It is against all the princes of Israel! They are given over to the sword with my people. Therefore strike your thigh in grief. [13] Surely it will be a trial! And what if the sword despises even the scepter? The scepter will not continue." This is the declaration of the Lord GOD.

[14] "So you, son of man, prophesy and clap your hands together:

Let the sword strike two times, even three.
It is a sword for massacre,
a sword for great massacre—
it surrounds them!
[15] I have appointed a sword for slaughter
at all their gates,
so that their hearts may melt
and many may stumble.
Yes! It is ready to flash like lightning;
it is drawn for slaughter.
[16] Slash to the right;
turn to the left—
wherever your blade is directed.

[17] I also will clap my hands together, and I will satisfy my wrath. I, the LORD, have spoken."

[18] The word of the LORD came to me: [19] "Now you, son of man, mark out two roads that the sword of Babylon's king can take. Both of them should originate from the same land. And make a signpost at the fork in the road to each city. [20] Mark out a road that the sword can take to Rabbah of the Ammonites and to Judah into fortified Jerusalem. [21] For the king of Babylon stands at the split in the road, at the fork of the two roads, to practice divination: he shakes the arrows, consults the idols, and observes the liver. [22] The answer marked Jerusalem appears in his right hand, indicating that he should set up battering rams, give the order to slaughter, raise a battle cry, set battering rams against the gates, build a ramp, and construct a siege wall. [23] It will seem like false divination to those who have sworn an oath to the Babylonians, but it will draw attention to their guilt so that they will be captured.

[24] "Therefore, this is what the Lord GOD says: Because you have drawn attention to your guilt, exposing your transgressions, so that your sins are revealed in all your actions—since you have done this, you will be captured by them. [25] And you, profane and wicked prince of Israel, the day has come for your punishment.

[26] "This is what the Lord GOD says:

Remove the turban, and take off the crown.
Things will not remain as they are;
exalt the lowly and bring down the exalted.
[27] A ruin, a ruin,
I will make it a ruin!
Yet this will not happen
until he comes;
I have given the judgment to him.

[28] "Now you, son of man, prophesy, and say, 'This is what the Lord GOD says concerning the Ammonites and their contempt.' You are to proclaim,

'A sword! A sword
is drawn for slaughter,
polished to consume, to flash like lightning.
[29] While they offer false visions
and lying divinations about you,
the time has come to put you
to the necks of the profane wicked ones;
the day has come
for final punishment.

[30] "'Return it to its sheath!
"'I will judge you
in the place where you were created,
in the land of your origin.
[31] I will pour out my indignation on you;
I will blow the fire of my fury on you.
I will hand you over to brutal men,
skilled at destruction.
[32] You will be fuel for the fire.
Your blood will be spilled within the land.
You will not be remembered,
for I, the LORD, have spoken.'"

● GOING DEEPER

1 PETER 3:18-21

[18] For Christ also suffered for sins once for all, the righteous for the unrighteous, that he might bring you to God. He was put to death in the flesh but made alive by the Spirit, [19] in which he also went and made proclamation to the spirits in prison [20] who in the past were disobedient, when God patiently waited in the days of Noah while the ark was being prepared. In it a few—that is, eight people—were saved through water. [21] Baptism, which corresponds to this, now saves you (not as the removal of dirt from the body, but the pledge of a good conscience toward God) through the resurrection of Jesus Christ…

An Indictment of Sinful Jerusalem

19

EZEKIEL 22

AN INDICTMENT OF SINFUL JERUSALEM

[1] The word of the LORD came to me: [2] "As for you, son of man, will you pass judgment? Will you pass judgment against the city of blood? Then explain all her detestable practices to her. [3] You are to say, 'This is what the Lord GOD says: A city that sheds blood within her walls so that her time of judgment has come and who makes idols for herself so that she is defiled! [4] You are guilty of the blood you have shed, and you are defiled from the idols you have made. You have brought your judgment days near and have come to your years of punishment. Therefore, I have made you a disgrace to the nations and a mockery to all the lands. [5] Those who are near and those far away from you will mock you, you infamous one full of turmoil.

[6] "'Look, every prince of Israel within you has used his strength to shed blood. [7] Father and mother are treated with contempt, and the resident alien is exploited within you. The fatherless and widow are oppressed in you. [8] You despise my holy things and profane my Sabbaths. [9] There are men within you who slander in order to shed blood. People who live in you eat at the mountain shrines; they commit depraved acts within you. [10] Men within you have sexual intercourse with their father's wife and violate women during their menstrual impurity. [11] One man within you commits a detestable act with his neighbor's wife; another defiles his daughter-in-law with depravity; and yet another violates his sister, his father's daughter. [12] People who live in you accept bribes in order to shed blood. You take interest and profit on a loan and brutally extort your neighbors. You have forgotten me. This is the declaration of the Lord GOD.

[13] "'Now look, I clap my hands together against the dishonest profit you have made and against the blood shed among you. [14] Will your courage endure or your hands be strong in the days when I deal with you?

I, THE LORD, HAVE SPOKEN, AND I WILL ACT.

[15] I will disperse you among the nations and scatter you among the countries; I will purge your uncleanness. [16] You will be profaned in the sight of the nations. Then you will know that I am the LORD.'"

JERUSALEM AS GOD'S FURNACE

[17] The word of the LORD came to me: [18] "Son of man, the house of Israel has become merely dross to me. All of them are copper, tin, iron, and lead inside the furnace; they are just dross from silver. [19] Therefore, this is what the Lord GOD says: Because all of you have become dross, I am about to gather you into Jerusalem. [20] Just as one gathers silver, copper, iron, lead, and tin into the furnace to blow fire on them and melt them, so I will gather you in my anger and wrath, put you inside, and melt you. [21] Yes, I will gather you together and blow on you with the fire of my fury, and you will be melted within the city. [22] As silver is melted inside a furnace, so you will be melted inside the city. Then you will know that I, the LORD, have poured out my wrath on you."

INDICTMENT OF A SINFUL LAND

[23] The word of the LORD came to me: [24] "Son of man, say to her, 'You are a land that has not been cleansed, that has not received rain in the day of indignation.' [25] The conspiracy of her prophets within her is like a roaring lion tearing its prey: they devour people, seize wealth and valuables, and multiply the widows within her. [26] Her priests do violence to my instruction and profane my holy things. They make no distinction between the holy and the common, and they do not explain the difference between the clean and the unclean. They close their eyes to my Sabbaths, and I am profaned among them.

[27] "Her officials within her are like wolves tearing their prey, shedding blood, and destroying lives in order to make profit dishonestly. [28] Her prophets plaster for them with whitewash by seeing false visions and lying divinations, saying, 'This is what the Lord GOD says,' when the LORD has not spoken. [29] The people of the land have practiced extortion and committed robbery. They have oppressed the poor and needy and unlawfully exploited the resident alien. [30] I searched for a man among them who would repair the wall and stand in the gap before me on behalf of the land so that I might not destroy it, but I found no one. [31] So I have poured out my indignation on them and consumed them with the fire of my fury. I have brought their conduct down on their own heads." This is the declaration of the Lord GOD.

EZEKIEL 23:1–27

THE TWO IMMORAL SISTERS

[1] The word of the LORD came to me again: [2] "Son of man, there were two women, daughters of the same mother, [3] who acted like prostitutes in Egypt, behaving promiscuously in their youth. Their breasts were fondled there, and their virgin nipples caressed. [4] The older one was named Oholah, and her sister was Oholibah. They became mine and gave birth to sons and daughters. As for their names, Oholah represents Samaria and Oholibah represents Jerusalem.

[5] "Oholah acted like a prostitute even though she was mine. She lusted after her lovers, the Assyrians: warriors [6] dressed in blue, governors and prefects, all of them desirable young men, horsemen riding on steeds. [7] She offered her sexual favors to them; all of them were the elite of Assyria. She defiled herself with all those she lusted after and with all their idols. [8] She didn't give up her promiscuity that began in Egypt, when men slept with her in her youth, caressed her virgin nipples, and poured out their lust on her. [9] Therefore, I handed her over to her lovers, the Assyrians she lusted for. [10] They exposed her nakedness, seized her sons and daughters, and killed her with the sword. Since they executed judgment against her, she became notorious among women.

[11] "Now her sister Oholibah saw this, but she was even more depraved in her lust than Oholah, and made her promiscuous acts worse than those of her sister. [12] She lusted after the Assyrians: governors and prefects, warriors splendidly dressed, horsemen riding on steeds, all of them desirable young men. [13] And I saw that she had defiled herself; both of them had taken the same path. [14] But she increased her promiscuity when she saw male figures carved on the wall, images of the Chaldeans, engraved in bright red, [15] wearing belts on their waists and flowing turbans on their heads; all of them looked like officers, a depiction of the Babylonians in Chaldea, their native land. [16] At the sight of them she lusted after them and sent messengers to them in Chaldea. [17] Then the Babylonians came to her, to the bed of love, and defiled her with their lust. But after she was defiled by them, she turned away from them in disgust. [18] When she flaunted her promiscuity and exposed her nakedness, I turned away from her in disgust just as I turned away from her sister. [19] Yet she multiplied her acts of promiscuity, remembering the days of her youth when she acted like a prostitute in the land of Egypt [20] and lusted after their lovers, whose sexual members were like those of donkeys and whose emission was like that of stallions. [21] So you revisited the depravity of your youth, when the Egyptians caressed your nipples to enjoy your youthful breasts.

[22] "Therefore, Oholibah, this is what the Lord GOD says: I am going to incite your lovers against you, those you turned away from in disgust. I will bring them against you from every side: [23] the Babylonians and all the Chaldeans; Pekod, Shoa, and Koa; and all the Assyrians with them—desirable young men, all of them governors and prefects, officers and administrators, all of them riding on steeds. [24] They will

come against you with an assembly of peoples and with weapons, chariots, and wagons. They will set themselves against you on every side with large and small shields and helmets. I will delegate judgment to them, and they will judge you by their own standards. ²⁵ When I vent my jealous fury on you, they will deal with you in wrath. They will cut off your nose and ears, and the rest of you will fall by the sword. They will seize your sons and daughters, and the rest of you will be consumed by fire. ²⁶ They will strip off your clothes and take your beautiful jewelry. ²⁷ So I will put an end to your depravity and sexual immorality, which began in the land of Egypt, and you will not look longingly at them or remember Egypt anymore."

🛡 GOING DEEPER

ROMANS 3:21-26

THE RIGHTEOUSNESS OF GOD THROUGH FAITH

²¹ But now, apart from the law, the righteousness of God has been revealed, attested by the Law and the Prophets. ²² The righteousness of God is through faith in Jesus Christ to all who believe, since there is no distinction. ²³ For all have sinned and fall short of the glory of God; ²⁴ they are justified freely by his grace through the redemption that is in Christ Jesus. ²⁵ God presented him as the mercy seat by his blood, through faith, to demonstrate his righteousness, because in his restraint God passed over the sins previously committed. ²⁶ God presented him to demonstrate his righteousness at the present time, so that he would be just and justify the one who has faith in Jesus.

Notes

Response

LAMENT

During this Lenten season, we make time to lament— to grieve our own sin and express sorrow over the brokenness of the world, to which our sin contributes.

1 What in your life do you need to lament? Take time to confess your own sin and grieve over how the sin of others has affected you.

2 How does your sin and brokenness affect your community? Take time to lament for the brokenness you see in the world.

CONFESSION
AND ASSURANCE

A lament is not a quick
fix, but God is faithful,
and lamenting gently but
persistently reminds us to
trust Him. Use this space to
confess your need for God
and His intervention, as well
as express your continued
hope found in His provision.

O Love That Will Not Let Me Go

WORDS
George Matheson

MUSIC
Albert L. Peace

1. O love that will not let me go, I rest my
2. O light that fol-l'west all my way, I yield my
3. O joy that seek-est me through pain, I can-not
4. O cross that lift-est up my head, I dare not

wea-ry soul in Thee; I give Thee back the life I owe, That
flick-'ring torch to Thee; My heart re-stores its bor-rowed ray, That
close my heart to Thee; I trace the rain-bow through the rain, And
ask to hide from thee; I lay in dust life's glo-ry dead, And

in Thine o-cean depths its flow may rich-er, full-er be.
in Thy sun-shine's glow its day may bright-er, fair-er be.
feel the prom-ise is not vain that morn shall tear-less be.
from the ground there blos-soms red, Life that shall end-less be.

GRACE DAY

The Lord does not delay his promise, as some understand delay, but is patient with you, not wanting any to perish but all to come to repentance.

2 PETER 3:9

DAY 20

Lent is a season where we reflect on the depth of our sin and embrace the hope and strength found only in the cross of Christ. We seek unhurried moments of quiet to read Scripture, pray, confess, and repent. Take some time today to catch up on your reading, make space for prayer, and rest in God's presence.

21 *Weekly Truth*

Scripture is God-breathed and true. When we memorize it, we carry His Word with us wherever we go.

This week we are continuing to commit Ezekiel 36:26–28 to memory by adding verse 27. God presents a promise in two parts: He will provide the presence of His Spirit, and His people will once again walk in His ways.

"I will give you a new heart and put a new spirit within you; I will remove your heart of stone and give you a heart of flesh. **I will place my Spirit within you and cause you to follow my statutes and carefully observe my ordinances.** You will live in the land that I gave your ancestors; you will be my people, and I will be your God."

EZEKIEL 36:26–28

See tips for memorizing Scripture on page 236.

"So you will be a sign for them, and they will know that I am the LORD."

EZEKIEL 24:27

The Death of Ezekiel's Wife

EZEKIEL 23:28–49

28 "For this is what the Lord God says: I am going to hand you over to those you hate, to those you turned away from in disgust. 29 They will treat you with hatred, take all you have worked for, and leave you stark naked, so that the shame of your debauchery will be exposed, both your depravity and promiscuity. 30 These things will be done to you because you acted like a prostitute with the nations, defiling yourself with their idols. 31 You have followed the path of your sister, so I will put her cup in your hand."

32 This is what the Lord God says:

"You will drink your sister's cup,
which is deep and wide.
You will be an object of ridicule and scorn,
for it holds so much.
33 You will be filled with drunkenness and grief,
with a cup of devastation and desolation,
the cup of your sister Samaria.
34 You will drink it and drain it;
then you will gnaw its broken pieces,
and tear your breasts.
For I have spoken."

This is the declaration of the Lord God.

35 Therefore, this is what the Lord God says: "Because you have forgotten me and cast me behind your back, you must bear the consequences of your indecency and promiscuity."

36 Then the Lord said to me, "Son of man, will you pass judgment against Oholah and Oholibah? Then declare their detestable practices to them. 37 For they have committed adultery, and blood is on their hands; they have committed adultery with their idols. And the children they bore to me they have sacrificed in the fire as food for the idols. 38 They also did this to me: they defiled my sanctuary on that same day and profaned my Sabbaths. 39 On the same day they slaughtered their children for their idols, they entered my sanctuary to profane it. Yes, that is what they did inside my house.

40 "In addition, they sent for men who came from far away when a messenger was dispatched to them. And look how they came! You bathed, painted your eyes, and adorned yourself with jewelry for them. 41 You sat on a luxurious couch with a table spread before it, on which you had set my incense and oil. 42 The sound of a carefree crowd was there. Drunkards from the desert were brought in, along with common men. They put bracelets on the women's hands and beautiful tiaras

SHE READS TRUTH   DAY 22   111

on their heads. [43] Then I said concerning this woman worn out by adultery: Will they now have illicit sex with her, even her? [44] Yet they had sex with her as one does with a prostitute. This is how they had sex with Oholah and Oholibah, those depraved women. [45] But righteous men will judge them the way adulteresses and those who shed blood are judged, for they are adulteresses and blood is on their hands.

[46] "This is what the Lord GOD says: Summon an assembly against them and consign them to terror and plunder. [47] The assembly will stone them and cut them down with their swords. They will kill their sons and daughters and burn their houses. [48] So I will put an end to depravity in the land, and all the women will be admonished not to imitate your depraved behavior. [49] They will punish you for your depravity, and you will bear the consequences for your sins of idolatry. Then you will know that I am the Lord GOD."

EZEKIEL 24

PARABLE OF THE BOILING POT

[1] The word of the LORD came to me in the ninth year, in the tenth month, on the tenth day of the month: [2] "Son of man, write down today's date, this very day. The king of Babylon has laid siege to Jerusalem this very day. [3] Now speak a parable to the rebellious house. Tell them, 'This is what the Lord GOD says:

Put the pot on the fire—
put it on,
and then pour water into it!
[4] Place the pieces of meat in it,
every good piece—
thigh and shoulder.
Fill it with choice bones.
[5] Take the choicest of the flock
and also pile up the fuel under it.
Bring it to a boil
and cook the bones in it.

[6] "'Therefore, this is what the Lord GOD says:

Woe to the city of bloodshed,
the pot that has corrosion inside it,

and its corrosion has not come out of it!
Empty it piece by piece;
lots should not be cast for its contents.
[7] For the blood she shed is still within her.
She put it out on the bare rock;
she didn't pour it on the ground
to cover it with dust.
[8] In order to stir up wrath and take vengeance,
I have put her blood on the bare rock,
so that it would not be covered.

[9] "'Therefore, this is what the Lord GOD says:

Woe to the city of bloodshed!
I myself will make the pile of kindling large.
[10] Pile on the logs and kindle the fire!
Cook the meat well
and mix in the spices!
Let the bones be burned!
[11] Set the empty pot on its coals
so that it becomes hot and its copper glows.
Then its impurity will melt inside it;
its corrosion will be consumed.
[12] It has frustrated every effort;
its thick corrosion will not come off.
Into the fire with its corrosion!
[13] Because of the depravity of your uncleanness—
since I tried to purify you,
but you would not be purified from your uncleanness—
you will not be pure again
until I have satisfied my wrath on you.
[14] I, the LORD, have spoken.
It is coming, and I will do it!
I will not refrain, I will not show pity,
and I will not relent.
I will judge you
according to your ways and deeds.

This is the declaration of the Lord GOD.'"

THE DEATH OF EZEKIEL'S WIFE: A SIGN

[15] Then the word of the LORD came to me: [16] "Son of man, I am about to take the delight of your eyes away from you with a fatal blow. But you must not lament or weep or let

your tears flow. [17] Groan quietly; do not observe mourning rites for the dead. Put on your turban and strap your sandals on your feet; do not cover your mustache or eat the bread of mourners."

[18] I spoke to the people in the morning, and my wife died in the evening. The next morning I did just as I was commanded. [19] Then the people asked me,

"WON'T YOU TELL US WHAT THESE THINGS YOU ARE DOING MEAN FOR US?"

[20] So I answered them: "The word of the LORD came to me, [21] Say to the house of Israel, 'This is what the Lord GOD says: I am about to desecrate my sanctuary, the pride of your power, the delight of your eyes, and the desire of your heart. Also, the sons and daughters you left behind will fall by the sword. [22] Then you will do just as I have done: You will not cover your mustache or eat the bread of mourners. [23] Your turbans will remain on your heads and your sandals on your feet. You will not lament or weep but will waste away because of your iniquities and will groan to one another. [24] Now Ezekiel will be a sign for you. You will do everything that he has done. When this happens, you will know that I am the Lord GOD.'

[25] "As for you, son of man, know that on that day I will take from them their stronghold—their pride and joy, the delight of their eyes, and the longing of their hearts—as well as their sons and daughters. [26] On that day a fugitive will come to you and report the news. [27] On that day your mouth will be opened to talk with him; you will speak and no longer be mute. So you will be a sign for them, and they will know that I am the LORD."

📖 GOING DEEPER

MATTHEW 1:21–23

[21] "She will give birth to a son, and you are to name him Jesus, because he will save his people from their sins."

[22] Now all this took place to fulfill what was spoken by the Lord through the prophet:

> [23] See, the virgin will become pregnant
> and give birth to a son,
> and they will name him Immanuel,

which is translated "God is with us."

HOW YOU HAVE PERISHED, CITY OF RENOWN. EZEKIEL 26:17

The Downfall of Tyre

EZEKIEL 25

PROPHECIES AGAINST THE NATIONS

JUDGMENT AGAINST AMMON

¹ Then the word of the LORD came to me: ² "Son of man, face the Ammonites and prophesy against them. ³ Say to the Ammonites, 'Hear the word of the Lord GOD: This is what the Lord GOD says: Because you said, "Aha!" about my sanctuary when it was desecrated, about the land of Israel when it was laid waste, and about the house of Judah when they went into exile, ⁴ therefore I am about to give you to the people of the east as a possession. They will set up their encampments and pitch their tents among you. They will eat your fruit and drink your milk. ⁵ I will make Rabbah a pasture for camels and Ammon a resting place for sheep. Then you will know that I am the LORD.

⁶ "'For this is what the Lord GOD says: Because you clapped your hands, stamped your feet, and rejoiced over the land of Israel with wholehearted contempt, ⁷ therefore I am about to stretch out my hand against you and give you as plunder to the nations. I will cut you off from the peoples and eliminate you from the countries. I will destroy you, and you will know that I am the LORD.

JUDGMENT AGAINST MOAB

⁸ "'This is what the Lord GOD says: Because Moab and Seir said, "Look, the house of Judah is like all the other nations." ⁹ Therefore I am about to expose Moab's flank beginning with its frontier cities, the splendor of the land: Beth-jeshimoth, Baal-meon, and Kiriathaim. ¹⁰ I will give it along with Ammon to the people of the east as a possession, so that Ammon will not be remembered among the nations. ¹¹ So I will execute judgments against Moab, and they will know that I am the LORD.

JUDGMENT AGAINST EDOM

¹² "'This is what the Lord GOD says: Because Edom acted vengefully against the house of Judah and incurred grievous guilt by taking revenge on them, ¹³ therefore this is what the Lord GOD says: I will stretch out my hand against Edom and cut off both people and animals from it. I will make it a wasteland; they will fall by the sword from Teman to Dedan. ¹⁴ I will take my vengeance on Edom through my people Israel, and they will deal with Edom according to my anger and wrath. So they will know my vengeance. This is the declaration of the Lord GOD.

JUDGMENT AGAINST PHILISTIA

¹⁵ "'This is what the Lord GOD says: Because the Philistines acted in vengeance and took revenge with deep contempt, destroying because of their perpetual hatred, ¹⁶ therefore this is what the Lord GOD says: I am about to stretch out my hand against the Philistines, cutting off the Cherethites and wiping out what remains of the coastal peoples. ¹⁷ I will execute severe vengeance against them with furious rebukes. They will know that I am the LORD when I take my vengeance on them.'"

EZEKIEL 26

THE DOWNFALL OF TYRE

[1] In the eleventh year, on the first day of the month, the word of the Lord came to me: [2] "Son of man, because Tyre said about Jerusalem, 'Aha! The gateway to the peoples is shattered. She has been turned over to me. I will be filled now that she lies in ruins,' [3] therefore this is what the Lord God says: See, I am against you, Tyre! I will raise up many nations against you, just as the sea raises its waves. [4] They will destroy the walls of Tyre and demolish her towers. I will scrape the soil from her and turn her into a bare rock. [5] She will become a place in the sea to spread nets, for I have spoken." This is the declaration of the Lord God. "She will become plunder for the nations, [6] and her villages on the mainland will be slaughtered by the sword. Then they will know that I am the Lord."

[7] For this is what the Lord God says: "See, I am about to bring King Nebuchadnezzar of Babylon, king of kings, against Tyre from the north with horses, chariots, cavalry, and a huge assembly of troops. [8] He will slaughter your villages on the mainland with the sword. He will set up siege works, build a ramp, and raise a wall of shields against you. [9] He will direct the blows of his battering rams against your walls and tear down your towers with his iron tools. [10] His horses will be so numerous that their dust will cover you. When he enters your gates as an army entering a breached city, your walls will shake from the noise of cavalry, wagons, and chariots. [11] He will trample all your streets with the hooves of his horses. He will slaughter your people with the sword, and your mighty pillars will fall to the ground. [12] They will take your wealth as spoil and plunder your merchandise. They will also demolish your walls and tear down your beautiful homes. Then they will throw your stones, timber, and soil into the water. [13] I will put an end to the noise of your songs, and the sound of your lyres will no longer be heard. [14] I will turn you into a bare rock, and you will be a place to spread nets. You will never be rebuilt, for I, the Lord, have spoken." This is the declaration of the Lord God.

[15] This is what the Lord God says to Tyre: "Won't the coasts and islands quake at the sound of your downfall, when the wounded groan and slaughter occurs within you? [16] All the princes of the sea will descend from their thrones, remove their robes, and strip off their embroidered garments. They will clothe themselves with trembling; they will sit on the ground, tremble continually, and be appalled at you. [17] Then they will lament for you and say of you,

'How you have perished, city of renown,
you who were populated from the seas!
She who was powerful on the sea,
she and all of her inhabitants
inflicted their terror.
[18] Now the coastlands tremble
on the day of your downfall;
the islands in the sea
are alarmed by your demise.'"

[19] For this is what the Lord God says: "When I make you a ruined city like other deserted cities, when I raise up the deep against you so that the mighty waters cover you, [20] then I will bring you down to be with those who descend to the Pit, to the people of antiquity. I will make you dwell in the underworld like the ancient ruins, with those who descend to the Pit, so that you will no longer be inhabited or display your splendor in the land of the living. [21] I will make you an object of horror, and you will no longer exist. You will be sought but will never be found again." This is the declaration of the Lord God.

🫛 GOING DEEPER

LUKE 10:13–16

UNREPENTANT TOWNS

[13] "Woe to you, Chorazin! Woe to you, Bethsaida! For if the miracles that were done in you had been done in Tyre and Sidon, they would have repented long ago, sitting in sackcloth and ashes. [14] But it will be more tolerable for Tyre and Sidon at the judgment than for you. [15] And you, Capernaum, will you be exalted to heaven? No, you will go down to Hades. [16] Whoever listens to you listens to me. Whoever rejects you rejects me. And whoever rejects me rejects the one who sent me."

Notes

Timeline of the Exile

Almost half of the Old Testament pertains to the Israelites' time as exiles in Assyria and Babylon, eras when God's people were removed from the promised land and forced to dwell among their captors as a result of their own disobedience to their covenant with God. Ezekiel's ministry took place specifically during the southern kingdom of Judah's exile in Babylon. This timeline provides an overview of key biblical events and people associated with the Jewish people's exile and return.

KEY	Biblical events for the exile and return
	Biblical figures

605 BC

Judean nobility and other princes are taken into captivity in Babylon's first siege

DN 1:1-7

Daniel, Shadrach, Meshach, and Abednego are among the nobles taken into captivity

734-732 BC

Israelites from Galilee, Gilead, and Naphtali are exiled to Assyria

2KG 15:29

Ezekiel is one of the exiles in this group

597 BC

More than ten thousand Judean officers, soldiers, and craftsmen are exiled from the promised land to the Babylonian Empire

2KG 24:10-17

700 BC

600 BC

722 BC

Israelites from the ten northern tribes are exiled to Assyria

2KG 17:1-6

Hoshea, the last king to reign in Israel, is arrested by the king of Assyria

640-609 BC

King Josiah of Judah, a faithful king who sought religous reform, reigns

605-586 BC

King Nebuchadnezzar of Babylon leads the invasions against Judah

Zerubbabel leads this
group back from exile
and helps oversee the
temple's construction

538 BC

After defeating Babylon,
King Cyrus of Persia issues
a decree allowing exiles
from Judah to return and
rebuild the temple

2CH 36:22-23
EZR 1-2

The prophet Ezra, who
sought to reestablish
worship in Jerusalem,
leads these exiles

536 BC

The foundation of
the new temple is
completed

EZR 3:10-13

458 BC

A second group of
exiles return from
Persia to Judah

EZR 7-8

515 BC

Second temple
construction is completed
and the Israelites
celebrate its dedication

EZR 6:15-22

500 BC

586 BC

Jerusalem is destroyed,
along with its temple
and city walls, and the
rest of Judah is taken
into captivity

2KG 25:11-12, 21
2CH 36:11-21

479-465 BC

Queen Esther reigns in
Persia after Jewish exiles
begin their return to Judah

Zedekiah, the last king to
reign in Judah, revolts against
Babylonian rule, resulting in
this destruction

Nehemiah leads this group and
oversees construction of the walls

444 BC

A third group of exiles
return and begin rebuilding
Jerusalem's walls

NEH 2

The Fall of Tyre's Ruler

EZEKIEL 27

THE SINKING OF TYRE

[1] The word of the LORD came to me: [2] "Now, son of man, lament for Tyre. [3] Say to Tyre, who is situated at the entrance of the sea, merchant of the peoples to many coasts and islands, 'This is what the Lord GOD says:

Tyre, you declared,
"I am perfect in beauty."
[4] Your realm was in the heart of the sea;
your builders perfected your beauty.
[5] They constructed all your planking
with pine trees from Senir.
They took a cedar from Lebanon
to make a mast for you.
[6] They made your oars of oaks from Bashan.
They made your deck of cypress wood
from the coasts of Cyprus,
inlaid with ivory.
[7] Your sail was made of
fine embroidered linen from Egypt,
and served as your banner.
Your awning was of blue and purple fabric
from the coasts of Elishah.
[8] The inhabitants of Sidon and Arvad
were your rowers.

Your wise men were within you, Tyre;
they were your captains.
[9] The elders of Gebal and its wise men
were within you, repairing your leaks.
"'All the ships of the sea and their sailors
came to you to barter for your goods.
[10] Men of Persia, Lud, and Put
were in your army, serving as your warriors.
They hung shields and helmets in you;
they gave you splendor.
[11] Men of Arvad and Helech
were stationed on your walls all around,
and Gammadites were in your towers.
They hung their shields all around your walls;
they perfected your beauty.

[12] "'Tarshish was your trading partner because of your abundant wealth of every kind. They exchanged silver, iron, tin, and lead for your merchandise. [13] Javan, Tubal, and Meshech were your merchants. They exchanged slaves and bronze utensils for your goods. [14] Those from Beth-togarmah exchanged horses, war horses, and mules for your merchandise. [15] Men of Dedan were also your merchants; many coasts and islands were your regular markets. They brought back ivory tusks and ebony as your payment. [16] Aram

was your trading partner because of your numerous products. They exchanged turquoise, purple and embroidered cloth, fine linen, coral, and rubies for your merchandise. ¹⁷ Judah and the land of Israel were your merchants. They exchanged wheat from Minnith, meal, honey, oil, and balm, for your goods. ¹⁸ Damascus was also your trading partner because of your numerous products and your abundant wealth of every kind, trading in wine from Helbon and white wool. ¹⁹ Vedan and Javan from Uzal dealt in your merchandise; wrought iron, cassia, and aromatic cane were exchanged for your goods. ²⁰ Dedan was your merchant in saddlecloths for riding. ²¹ Arabia and all the princes of Kedar were your business partners, trading with you in lambs, rams, and goats. ²² The merchants of Sheba and Raamah traded with you. For your merchandise they exchanged the best of all spices and all kinds of precious stones as well as gold. ²³ Haran, Canneh, Eden, the merchants of Sheba, Asshur, and Chilmad traded with you. ²⁴ They were your merchants in choice garments, cloaks of blue and embroidered materials, and multicolored carpets, which were bound and secured with cords in your marketplace. ²⁵ Ships of Tarshish were the carriers for your goods.

"'So you became full and heavily loaded
in the heart of the sea.
²⁶ Your rowers have brought you
onto the high seas,
but the east wind has wrecked you
in the heart of the sea.
²⁷ Your wealth, merchandise, and goods,
your sailors and captains,
those who repair your leaks,
those who barter for your goods,
and all the warriors on board,
with all the other people within you,
sink into the heart of the sea
on the day of your downfall.

²⁸ "'The countryside shakes
at the sound of your sailors' cries.
²⁹ All the oarsmen
disembark from their ships.
The sailors and all the captains of the sea
stand on the shore.

³⁰ Because of you, they raise their voices
and cry out bitterly.
They throw dust on their heads;
they roll in ashes.
³¹ They shave their heads because of you
and wrap themselves in sackcloth.
They weep over you
with deep anguish and bitter mourning.

³² "'In their wailing they lament for you,
mourning over you:
"Who was like Tyre,
silenced in the middle of the sea?
³³ When your merchandise was unloaded from the seas,
you satisfied many peoples.
You enriched the kings of the earth
with your abundant wealth and goods.
³⁴ Now you are wrecked by the sea
in the depths of the waters;
your goods and the people within you
have gone down.
³⁵ All the inhabitants of the coasts and islands
are appalled at you.
Their kings shudder with fear;
their faces are contorted.
³⁶ Those who trade among the peoples
scoff at you;
you have become an object of horror
and will never exist again."'"

EZEKIEL 28

THE FALL OF TYRE'S RULER

¹ The word of the LORD came to me: ² "Son of man, say to the ruler of Tyre, 'This is what the Lord GOD says: Your heart is proud, and you have said, "I am a god; I sit in the seat of gods in the heart of the sea." Yet you are a man and not a god, though you have regarded your heart as that of a god. ³ Yes, you are wiser than Daniel; no secret is hidden from you! ⁴ By your wisdom and understanding you have acquired wealth for yourself. You have acquired gold and silver for your treasuries. ⁵ By your great skill in trading you have increased your wealth, but your heart has become proud because of your wealth.

6 "'Therefore, this is what the Lord GOD says:

Because you regard your heart as that of a god,
7 I am about to bring strangers against you,
ruthless men from the nations.
They will draw their swords
against your magnificent wisdom
and will pierce your splendor.
8 They will bring you down to the Pit,
and you will die a violent death
in the heart of the sea.
9 Will you still say, "I am a god,"
in the presence of those who slay you?
Yet you will be only a man, not a god,
in the hands of those who kill you.
10 You will die the death of the uncircumcised
at the hands of strangers.
For I have spoken.

This is the declaration of the Lord GOD.'"

A LAMENT FOR TYRE'S KING

11 The word of the LORD came to me: 12 "Son of man, lament for the king of Tyre and say to him, 'This is what the Lord GOD says:

YOU WERE THE SEAL OF PERFECTION, FULL OF WISDOM AND PERFECT IN BEAUTY.

13 You were in Eden, the garden of God.
Every kind of precious stone covered you:
carnelian, topaz, and diamond,
beryl, onyx, and jasper,
lapis lazuli, turquoise and emerald.
Your mountings and settings were crafted in gold;
they were prepared on the day you were created.
14 You were an anointed guardian cherub,
for I had appointed you.
You were on the holy mountain of God;
you walked among the fiery stones.
15 From the day you were created
you were blameless in your ways
until wickedness was found in you.

16 Through the abundance of your trade,
you were filled with violence, and you sinned.
So I expelled you in disgrace
from the mountain of God,
and banished you, guardian cherub,
from among the fiery stones.
17 Your heart became proud because of your beauty;
For the sake of your splendor
you corrupted your wisdom.
So I threw you down to the ground;
I made you a spectacle before kings.
18 You profaned your sanctuaries
by the magnitude of your iniquities
in your dishonest trade.
So I made fire come from within you,
and it consumed you.
I reduced you to ashes on the ground
in the sight of everyone watching you.
19 All those who know you among the peoples
are appalled at you.
You have become an object of horror
and will never exist again.'"

A PROPHECY AGAINST SIDON

20 The word of the LORD came to me: 21 "Son of man, face Sidon and prophesy against it. 22 You are to say, 'This is what the Lord GOD says:

Look! I am against you, Sidon,
and I will display my glory within you.
They will know that I am the LORD
when I execute judgments against her
and demonstrate my holiness through her.
23 I will send a plague against her
and bloodshed in her streets;
the slain will fall within her,
while the sword is against her on every side.
Then they will know that I am the LORD.

24 "'The house of Israel will no longer be hurt by prickly briers or painful thorns from all their neighbors who treat them with contempt. Then they will know that I am the Lord GOD.

Notes

25 "'This is what the Lord God says: When I gather the house of Israel from the peoples where they are scattered, I will demonstrate my holiness through them in the sight of the nations, and they will live in their own land, which I gave to my servant Jacob. 26 They will live there securely, build houses, and plant vineyards. They will live securely when I execute judgments against all their neighbors who treat them with contempt. Then they will know that I am the Lord their God.'"

🛡 GOING DEEPER

PSALM 106:47

Save us, Lord our God,
and gather us from the nations,
so that we may give thanks to your holy name
and rejoice in your praise.

REVELATION 21:23–27

23 The city does not need the sun or the moon to shine on it, because the glory of God illuminates it, and its lamp is the Lamb. 24 The nations will walk by its light, and the kings of the earth will bring their glory into it. 25 Its gates will never close by day because it will never be night there. 26 They will bring the glory and honor of the nations into it. 27 Nothing unclean will ever enter it, nor anyone who does what is detestable or false, but only those written in the Lamb's book of life.

A Prophecy of Egypt's Ruin

25

A PROPHECY OF EGYPT'S RUIN

[1] In the tenth year, in the tenth month on the twelfth day of the month, the word of the LORD came to me: [2] "Son of man, face Pharaoh king of Egypt and prophesy against him and against all of Egypt. [3] Speak to him and say, 'This is what the Lord GOD says:

Look, I am against you, Pharaoh king of Egypt,
the great monster lying in the middle of his Nile,
who says, "My Nile is my own;
I made it for myself."
[4] I will put hooks in your jaws
and make the fish of your streams
cling to your scales.
I will haul you up
from the middle of your Nile,
and all the fish of your streams
will cling to your scales.
[5] I will leave you in the desert,
you and all the fish of your streams.
You will fall on the open ground
and will not be taken away
or gathered for burial.
I have given you
to the wild creatures of the earth
and the birds of the sky as food.

[6] "'Then all the inhabitants of Egypt
will know that I am the LORD,
for they have been a staff made of reed
to the house of Israel.

[7] When Israel grasped you by the hand,
you splintered, tearing all their shoulders;
when they leaned on you,
you shattered and made all their hips unsteady.

[8] "'Therefore, this is what the Lord GOD says: I am going to bring a sword against you and cut off both people and animals from you.

[9] THE LAND OF EGYPT WILL BE A DESOLATE RUIN. THEN THEY WILL KNOW THAT I AM THE LORD.

Because you said, "The Nile is my own; I made it," [10] therefore, I am against you and your Nile. I will turn the land of Egypt into ruins, a desolate waste from Migdol to Syene, as far as the border of Cush. [11] No human foot will pass through it, and no animal foot will pass through it. It will be uninhabited for forty years. [12] I will make the land of Egypt a desolation among desolate lands, and its cities will be a desolation among ruined cities for forty years. I will disperse the Egyptians among the nations and scatter them throughout the lands.

[13] "'For this is what the Lord GOD says: At the end of forty years I will gather the Egyptians from the peoples where they were dispersed. [14] I will restore the fortunes of Egypt and bring them back to the land of Pathros, the land of their origin. There they will be a lowly kingdom. [15] Egypt will be the lowliest of kingdoms and will never again exalt itself over the nations. I will make them so small they cannot rule over the nations. [16] It will never again be an object of trust for the house of Israel, drawing attention to their iniquity of turning to the Egyptians. Then they will know that I am the Lord GOD.'"

BABYLON RECEIVES EGYPT AS COMPENSATION

[17] In the twenty-seventh year, in the first month, on the first day of the month, the word of the LORD came to me: [18] "Son of man, King Nebuchadnezzar of Babylon made his army labor strenuously against Tyre. Every head was made bald and every shoulder chafed, but he and his army received no compensation from Tyre for the labor he expended against it. [19] Therefore, this is what the Lord GOD says: I am going to give the land of Egypt to King Nebuchadnezzar of Babylon, and he will carry off its wealth, seizing its spoil and taking its plunder. This will be his army's compensation. [20] I have given him the land of Egypt as the pay he labored for, since they worked for me." This is the declaration of the Lord GOD.

21 "In that day I will cause a horn to sprout for the house of Israel, and I will enable you to speak out among them. Then they will know that I am the Lord."

EZEKIEL 30

EGYPT'S DOOM

1 The word of the Lord came to me: 2 "Son of man, prophesy and say, 'This is what the Lord God says:

Wail, "Woe because of that day!"
3 For a day is near;
a day belonging to the Lord is near.
It will be a day of clouds,
a time of doom for the nations.
4 A sword will come against Egypt,
and there will be anguish in Cush
when the slain fall in Egypt,
and its wealth is taken away,
and its foundations are demolished.
5 Cush, Put, and Lud,
and all the various foreign troops,
plus Libya and the men of the covenant land
will fall by the sword along with them.
6 This is what the Lord says:
Those who support Egypt will fall,
and its proud strength will collapse.
From Migdol to Syene
they will fall within it by the sword.
    This is the declaration of the Lord God.
7 They will be desolate
among desolate lands,
and their cities will lie
among ruined cities.
8 They will know that I am the Lord
when I set fire to Egypt
and all its allies are shattered.

9 On that day, messengers will go out from me in ships to terrify confident Cush. Anguish will come over them on the day of Egypt's doom. For indeed it is coming.

10 "'This is what the Lord God says:

I will put an end to the hordes of Egypt
by the hand of King Nebuchadnezzar of Babylon.
11 He along with his people,
ruthless men from the nations,
will be brought in to destroy the land.
They will draw their swords against Egypt
and fill the land with the slain.
12 I will make the streams dry
and sell the land to evil men.
I will bring desolation
on the land and everything in it
by the hands of foreigners.
I, the Lord, have spoken.

13 "'This is what the Lord God says:

I WILL DESTROY THE WORTHLESS IDOLS
AND PUT AN END TO THE FALSE GODS
   IN MEMPHIS.
THERE WILL NO LONGER BE
A PRINCE FROM THE LAND OF EGYPT.
AND I WILL INSTILL FEAR IN THAT LAND.

14 I will make Pathros desolate,
set fire to Zoan,
and execute judgments on Thebes.
15 I will pour out my wrath on Pelusium,
the stronghold of Egypt,
and will wipe out the hordes of Thebes.
16 I will set fire to Egypt;
Pelusium will writhe in anguish,
Thebes will be breached,
and Memphis will face foes in broad daylight.
17 The young men of On and Pi-beseth
will fall by the sword,
and those cities will go into captivity.
18 The day will be dark in Tehaphnehes,
when I break the yoke of Egypt there
and its proud strength
comes to an end in the city.
A cloud will cover Tehaphnehes,
and its surrounding villages will go into captivity.
19 So I will execute judgments against Egypt,
and they will know that I am the Lord.'"

PHARAOH'S POWER BROKEN

[20] In the eleventh year, in the first month, on the seventh day of the month, the word of the LORD came to me: [21] "Son of man, I have broken the arm of Pharaoh king of Egypt. Look, it has not been bandaged—no medicine has been applied and no splint put on to bandage it so that it can grow strong enough to handle a sword. [22] Therefore, this is what the Lord GOD says: Look! I am against Pharaoh king of Egypt. I will break his arms, both the strong one and the one already broken, and will make the sword fall from his hand. [23] I will disperse the Egyptians among the nations and scatter them among the countries. [24] I will strengthen the arms of Babylon's king and place my sword in his hand. But I will break the arms of Pharaoh, and he will groan before him as a mortally wounded man. [25] I will strengthen the arms of Babylon's king, but Pharaoh's arms will fall. They will know that I am the LORD when I place my sword in the hand of Babylon's king and he wields it against the land of Egypt. [26] When I disperse the Egyptians among the nations and scatter them among the countries, they will know that I am the LORD."

♥ GOING DEEPER

ROMANS 5:6–11

THE JUSTIFIED ARE RECONCILED

[6] For while we were still helpless, at the right time, Christ died for the ungodly. [7] For rarely will someone die for a just person—though for a good person perhaps someone might even dare to die. [8] But God proves his own love for us in that while we were still sinners, Christ died for us. [9] How much more then, since we have now been justified by his blood, will we be saved through him from wrath. [10] For if, while we were enemies, we were reconciled to God through the death of his Son, then how much more, having been reconciled, will we be saved by his life. [11] And not only that, but we also boast in God through our Lord Jesus Christ, through whom we have now received this reconciliation.

"You are my flock, the human flock

of my pasture, and I am your God."

EZEKIEL 34:31

A Lament for Pharaoh

DAY 26

DOWNFALL OF EGYPT AND ASSYRIA

[1] In the eleventh year, in the third month, on the first day of the month, the word of the LORD came to me: [2] "Son of man, say to Pharaoh king of Egypt and to his hordes,

'Who are you like in your greatness?
[3] Think of Assyria, a cedar in Lebanon,
with beautiful branches and shady foliage
and of lofty height.
Its top was among the clouds.
[4] The waters caused it to grow;
the underground springs made it tall,
directing their rivers all around
the place where the tree was planted
and sending their channels
to all the trees of the field.
[5] Therefore the cedar became greater in height
than all the trees of the field.
Its branches multiplied,
and its boughs grew long
as it spread them out
because of the abundant water.
[6] All the birds of the sky
nested in its branches,
and all the animals of the field
gave birth beneath its boughs;
all the great nations lived in its shade.
[7] It was beautiful in its size,
in the length of its limbs,
for its roots extended to abundant water.
[8] The cedars in God's garden could not eclipse it;
the pine trees couldn't compare with its branches,
nor could the plane trees match its boughs.
No tree in the garden of God
could compare with it in beauty.

[9] I made it beautiful with its many limbs,
and all the trees of Eden,
which were in God's garden, envied it.

[10] "'Therefore, this is what the Lord GOD says: Since it towered high in stature and set its top among the clouds, and it grew proud on account of its height, [11] I determined

to hand it over to a ruler of nations; he would surely deal with it. I banished it because of its wickedness. ¹² Foreigners, ruthless men from the nations, cut it down and left it lying. Its limbs fell on the mountains and in every valley; its boughs lay broken in all the earth's ravines. All the peoples of the earth left its shade and abandoned it. ¹³ All the birds of the sky nested on its fallen trunk, and all the animals of the field were among its boughs. ¹⁴ This happened so that no trees planted beside water would become great in height and set their tops among the clouds, and so that no other well-watered trees would reach them in height. For they have all been consigned to death, to the underworld, among the people who descend to the Pit.

¹⁵ "'This is what the Lord God says: I caused grieving on the day the cedar went down to Sheol. I closed off the underground deep because of it: I held back the rivers of the deep, and its abundant water was restrained. I made Lebanon mourn on account of it, and all the trees of the field fainted because of it. ¹⁶ I made the nations quake at the sound of its downfall, when I threw it down to Sheol to be with those who descend to the Pit. Then all the trees of Eden, the choice and best of Lebanon, all the well-watered trees, were comforted in the underworld. ¹⁷ They too descended with it to Sheol, to those slain by the sword. As its allies they had lived in its shade among the nations.

¹⁸ "'Who then are you like in glory and greatness among Eden's trees? You also will be brought down to the underworld to be with the trees of Eden. You will lie among the uncircumcised with those slain by the sword. This is Pharaoh and all his hordes. This is the declaration of the Lord God.'"

EZEKIEL 32

A LAMENT FOR PHARAOH

¹ In the twelfth year, in the twelfth month, on the first day of the month, the word of the Lord came to me: ² "Son of man, lament for Pharaoh king of Egypt and say to him,

'You compare yourself to a lion of the nations,
but you are like a monster in the seas.
You thrash about in your rivers,

churn up the waters with your feet,
and muddy the rivers.

³ "'This is what the Lord God says:

I will spread my net over you
with an assembly of many peoples,
and they will haul you up in my net.
⁴ I will abandon you on the land
and throw you onto the open field.
I will cause all the birds of the sky
to settle on you
and let the wild creatures of the entire earth
eat their fill of you.
⁵ I will put your flesh on the mountains
and fill the valleys with your carcass.
⁶ I will drench the land
with the flow of your blood,
even to the mountains;
the ravines will be filled with your gore.
⁷ "'When I snuff you out,
I will cover the heavens
and darken their stars.
I will cover the sun with a cloud,
and the moon will not give its light.
⁸ I will darken all the shining lights
in the heavens over you,
and will bring darkness on your land.
    This is the declaration of the Lord God.
⁹ "'I will trouble the hearts of many peoples,
when I bring about your destruction
among the nations,
in countries you have not known.
¹⁰ I will cause many peoples to be appalled at you,
and their kings will shudder with fear because of you
when I brandish my sword in front of them.
On the day of your downfall
each of them will tremble
every moment for his life.

¹¹ "'For this is what the Lord God says:

The sword of Babylon's king
will come against you!

¹² I will make your hordes fall
by the swords of warriors,
all of them ruthless men from the nations.
They will ravage Egypt's pride,
and all its hordes will be destroyed.
¹³ I will slaughter all its cattle
that are beside many waters.
No human foot will churn them again,
and no cattle hooves will disturb them.
¹⁴ Then I will let their waters settle
and will make their rivers flow like oil.
   This is the declaration of the Lord God.
¹⁵ When I make the land of Egypt a desolation,
so that it is emptied of everything in it,
when I strike down all who live there,
then they will know that I am the Lord.

¹⁶ "'The daughters of the nations will chant that lament. They will chant it over Egypt and all its hordes. This is the declaration of the Lord God.'"

EGYPT IN SHEOL

¹⁷ In the twelfth year, on the fifteenth day of the month, the word of the Lord came to me: ¹⁸ "Son of man, wail over the hordes of Egypt and bring Egypt and the daughters of mighty nations down to the underworld, to be with those who descend to the Pit:

¹⁹ Who do you surpass in loveliness?
Go down and be laid to rest with the uncircumcised!
²⁰ They will fall among those slain by the sword.
A sword is appointed!
They drag her and all her hordes away.
²¹ Warrior leaders will speak
from the middle of Sheol
about him and his allies:
'They have come down;
the uncircumcised lie
slain by the sword.'

²² "Assyria is there with her whole assembly;
her graves are all around her.
All of them are slain, fallen by the sword.

²³ Her graves are set in the deepest regions of the Pit,
and her assembly is all around her burial place.
All of them are slain, fallen by the sword—
those who once spread terror
in the land of the living.

²⁴ "Elam is there
with all her hordes around her grave.
All of them are slain, fallen by the sword—
those who went down to the underworld uncircumcised,
who once spread their terror
in the land of the living.
They bear their disgrace
with those who descend to the Pit.
²⁵ Among the slain
they prepare a bed for Elam
with all her hordes.
Her graves are all around her.
All of them are uncircumcised,
slain by the sword,
although their terror was once spread
in the land of the living.
They bear their disgrace
with those who descend to the Pit.
They are placed among the slain.

²⁶ "Meshech and Tubal are there,
with all their hordes.
Their graves are all around them.
All of them are uncircumcised, slain by the sword,
although their terror was once spread
in the land of the living.
²⁷ They do not lie down
with the fallen warriors of the uncircumcised,
who went down to Sheol
with their weapons of war,
whose swords were placed under their heads
and their shields
rested on their bones,
although the terror of these warriors
was once in the land of the living.
²⁸ But you will be shattered
and will lie down among the uncircumcised,
with those slain by the sword.

²⁹ "Edom is there, her kings and all her princes,
who, despite their strength, have been placed
among those slain by the sword.
They lie down with the uncircumcised,
with those who descend to the Pit.
³⁰ All the leaders of the north
and all the Sidonians are there.
They went down in shame with the slain,
despite the terror their strength inspired.
They lie down uncircumcised
with those slain by the sword.
They bear their disgrace
with those who descend to the Pit.

³¹ "Pharaoh will see them
and be comforted over all his hordes—
Pharaoh and his whole army,
slain by the sword."

This is the declaration of the Lord God.

³² "For I will spread my terror
in the land of the living,
so Pharaoh and all his hordes
will be laid to rest among the uncircumcised,
with those slain by the sword."

This is the declaration of the Lord God.

◆ GOING DEEPER

1 CORINTHIANS 1:26–31

BOASTING ONLY IN THE LORD

²⁶ Brothers and sisters, consider your calling: Not many were wise from a human perspective, not many powerful, not many of noble birth. ²⁷ Instead, God has chosen what is foolish in the world to shame the wise, and God has chosen what is weak in the world to shame the strong. ²⁸ God has chosen what is insignificant and despised in the world—what is viewed as nothing—to bring to nothing what is viewed as something, ²⁹ so that no one may boast in his presence. ³⁰ It is from him that you are in Christ Jesus, who became wisdom from God for us—our righteousness, sanctification, and redemption— ³¹ in order that, as it is written: Let the one who boasts, boast in the Lord.

Response

LAMENT

During this Lenten season, we make time to lament— to grieve our own sin and express sorrow over the brokenness of the world, to which our sin contributes.

1   What in your life do you need to lament? Take time to confess your own sin and grieve over how the sin of others has affected you.

2   How does your sin and brokenness affect your community? Take time to lament for the brokenness you see in the world.

CONFESSION
AND ASSURANCE

A lament is not a quick
fix, but God is faithful,
and lamenting gently but
persistently reminds us to
trust Him. Use this space to
confess your need for God
and His intervention, as well
as express your continued
hope found in His provision.

Lemon Lavender Bundt Cakes

MAKES 12 CAKES

INGREDIENTS

3 cups blanched almond flour

½ cup arrowroot powder

2 tablespoons dried lavender

⅓ cup palm shortening, melted

¼ cup light-colored raw honey

¼ cup almond milk

¼ cup freshly squeezed lemon juice

1 tablespoon finely grated lemon zest

1 teaspoon pure vanilla extract

4 eggs, at room temperature

1 teaspoon baking soda

¼ teaspoon fine sea salt

GLAZE

3 tablespoons light-colored raw honey

1 teaspoon freshly squeezed lemon juice

1 teaspoon dried lavender

½ teaspoon finely grated lemon zest

½ cup coconut butter

¼ cup water

DIRECTIONS

Preheat the oven to 325°F. Grease two 6-cavity mini silicone Bundt pans well with palm shortening and place them on a baking sheet.

Combine the almond flour, arrowroot powder, and lavender in a food processor and process for 15 seconds, or until finely ground. Add the palm shortening, honey, almond milk, lemon juice, lemon zest, and vanilla and process until well combined. Add the eggs, one at a time, blending after each addition until incorporated. Add the baking soda and salt and process again until combined. Pour the batter into the prepared pans.

Bake for 20 to 25 minutes, until a toothpick inserted into the center comes out clean. Cool on a wire rack for 15 minutes, then gently release the cakes from the pans and cool completely.

To make the glaze, heat the honey, lemon juice, lavender, and lemon zest in a small saucepan over medium heat. Simmer for 5 minutes, then remove from the heat and whisk in the coconut butter and water until smooth. Dip the top of each cake in the glaze, then place the cakes in the refrigerator for 20 minutes to set. Serve immediately or store the cakes tightly wrapped in the refrigerator for up to 5 days.

GRACE DAY

Save us, LORD our God, and gather
us from the nations, so that we
may give thanks to your holy name
and rejoice in your praise.

PSALM 106:47

DAY 27

Lent is a season where we reflect on the depth of our sin and embrace the
hope and strength found only in the cross of Christ. We seek unhurried
moments of quiet to read Scripture, pray, confess, and repent. Take some
time today to catch up on your reading, make space for prayer, and rest in
God's presence.

28

Weekly Truth

Scripture is God-breathed and true. When we memorize it, we carry His Word with us wherever we go.

This week we add the final verse to our memorization of God's promise of restoration in Ezekiel 36:26–28. In verse 28, God reminds Israel of the covenant He made with them and promises to fulfill it.

"I will give you a new heart and put a new spirit within you; I will remove your heart of stone and give you a heart of flesh. I will place my Spirit within you and cause you to follow my statutes and carefully observe my ordinances. **You will live in the land that I gave your ancestors; you will be my people, and I will be your God.**"

EZEKIEL 36:26–28

EZEKIEL 36:28

See tips for memorizing Scripture on page 236.

"I take no pleasure in the death of the wicked, but rather that the wicked person should turn from his way and live."

EZEKIEL 33:11

Ezekiel As the Lord's Messenger

EZEKIEL 33

EZEKIEL AS ISRAEL'S WATCHMAN

[1] The word of the LORD came to me: [2] "Son of man, speak to your people and tell them, 'Suppose I bring the sword against a land, and the people of that land select a man from among them, appointing him as their watchman. [3] And suppose he sees the sword coming against the land and blows his ram's horn to warn the people. [4] Then, if anyone hears the sound of the ram's horn but ignores the warning, and the sword comes and takes him away, his death will be his own fault. [5] Since he heard the sound of the ram's horn but ignored the warning, his death is his own fault. If he had taken warning, he would have saved his life. [6] However, suppose the watchman sees the sword coming but doesn't blow the ram's horn, so that the people aren't warned, and the sword comes and takes away their lives. Then they have been taken away because of their iniquity, but I will hold the watchman accountable for their blood.'

[7] "As for you, son of man, I have made you a watchman for the house of Israel. When you hear a word from my mouth, give them a warning from me. [8] If I say to the wicked, 'Wicked one, you will surely die,' but you do not speak out to warn him about his way, that wicked person will die for his iniquity, yet I will hold you responsible for his blood. [9] But if you warn a wicked person to turn from his way and he doesn't turn from it, he will die for his iniquity, but you will have rescued yourself.

[10] "Now as for you, son of man, say to the house of Israel, 'You have said this: "Our transgressions and our sins are heavy on us, and we are wasting away because of them! How then can we survive?"' [11] Tell them, 'As I live—this is the declaration of the Lord GOD—I take no pleasure in the death of the wicked, but rather that the wicked person should turn from his way and live. Repent, repent of your evil ways! Why will you die, house of Israel?'

[12] "Now, son of man, say to your people, 'The righteousness of the righteous person will not save him on the day of his transgression; neither will the wickedness of the wicked person cause him to stumble on the day he turns from his wickedness. The righteous person won't be able to survive by his righteousness on the day he sins. [13] When I tell the righteous person that he will surely live, but he trusts in his righteousness and acts unjustly, then none of his righteousness will be remembered, and he will die because of the injustice he has committed.

[14] "'So when I tell the wicked person, "You will surely die," but he repents of his sin and does what is just and right— [15] he returns collateral, makes restitution for what he has stolen, and walks in the statutes of life without committing injustice—he will certainly live; he will not die. [16] None of the sins he committed will be held against him. He has done what is just and right; he will certainly live.

17 "'But your people say, "The Lord's way isn't fair," even though it is their own way that isn't fair. 18 When a righteous person turns from his righteousness and commits injustice, he will die for it. 19 But if a wicked person turns from his wickedness and does what is just and right, he will live because of it. 20 Yet you say, "The Lord's way isn't fair." I will judge each of you according to his ways, house of Israel.'"

THE NEWS OF JERUSALEM'S FALL

21 In the twelfth year of our exile, in the tenth month, on the fifth day of the month, a fugitive from Jerusalem came to me and reported, "The city has been taken!" 22 Now the hand of the Lord had been on me the evening before the fugitive arrived, and he opened my mouth before the man came to me in the morning. So my mouth was opened and I was no longer mute.

ISRAEL'S CONTINUED REBELLION

23 Then the word of the Lord came to me: 24 "Son of man, those who live in the ruins in the land of Israel are saying, 'Abraham was only one person, yet he received possession of the land. But we are many; surely the land has been given to us as a possession.' 25 Therefore say to them, 'This is what the Lord God says: You eat meat with blood in it, you look to your idols, and you shed blood. Should you then receive possession of the land? 26 You have relied on your swords, you have committed detestable acts, and each of you has defiled his neighbor's wife. Should you then receive possession of the land?'

27 "Tell them this: 'This is what the Lord God says: As surely as I live, those who are in the ruins will fall by the sword, those in the open field I have given to wild animals to be devoured, and those in the strongholds and caves will die by plague. 28 I will make the land a desolate waste, and its proud strength will come to an end. The mountains of Israel will become desolate, with no one passing through. 29 They will know that I am the Lord when I make the land a desolate waste because of all the detestable acts they have committed.'

30 "As for you, son of man, your people are talking about you near the city walls and in the doorways of their houses. One person speaks to another, each saying to his brother, 'Come

and hear what the message is that comes from the Lord!' 31 So my people come to you in crowds, sit in front of you, and hear your words, but they don't obey them. Their mouths go on passionately, but their hearts pursue dishonest profit. 32 Yes, to them you are like a singer of passionate songs who has a beautiful voice and plays skillfully on an instrument. They hear your words, but they don't obey them. 33 Yet when all this comes true—and it definitely will—then they will know that a prophet has been among them."

♥ GOING DEEPER

ROMANS 5:1-5

FAITH TRIUMPHS

1 Therefore, since we have been justified by faith, we have peace with God through our Lord Jesus Christ. 2 We have also obtained access through him by faith into this grace in which we stand, and we boast in the hope of the glory of God. 3 And not only that, but we also boast in our afflictions, because we know that affliction produces endurance, 4 endurance produces proven character, and proven character produces hope. 5 This hope will not disappoint us, because God's love has been poured out in our hearts through the Holy Spirit who was given to us.

EPHESIANS 4:11-16

11 And he himself gave some to be apostles, some prophets, some evangelists, some pastors and teachers, 12 to equip the saints for the work of ministry, to build up the body of Christ, 13 until we all reach unity in the faith and in the knowledge of God's Son, growing into maturity with a stature measured by Christ's fullness. 14 Then we will no longer be little children, tossed by the waves and blown around by every wind of teaching, by human cunning with cleverness in the techniques of deceit. 15 But speaking the truth in love, let us grow in every way into him who is the head—Christ. 16 From him the whole body, fitted and knit together by every supporting ligament, promotes the growth of the body for building itself up in love by the proper working of each individual part.

Notes

The Shepherds and God's Flock

EZEKIEL 34

THE SHEPHERDS AND GOD'S FLOCK

1 The word of the LORD came to me: 2 "Son of man, prophesy against the shepherds of Israel. Prophesy, and say to them, 'This is what the Lord GOD says to the shepherds: Woe to the shepherds of Israel, who have been feeding themselves! Shouldn't the shepherds feed their flock? 3 You eat the fat, wear the wool, and butcher the fattened animals, but you do not tend the flock. 4 You have not strengthened the weak, healed the sick, bandaged the injured, brought back the strays, or sought the lost. Instead, you have ruled them with violence and cruelty. 5 They were scattered for lack of a shepherd; they became food for all the wild animals when they were scattered. 6 My flock went astray on all the mountains and every high hill. My flock was scattered over the whole face of the earth, and there was no one searching or seeking for them.

7 "'Therefore, you shepherds, hear the word of the LORD. 8 As I live—this is the declaration of the Lord GOD—because my flock, lacking a shepherd, has become prey and food for every wild animal, and because my shepherds do not search for my flock, and because the shepherds feed themselves rather than my flock, 9 therefore, you shepherds, hear the word of the LORD!

10 "'This is what the Lord GOD says: Look, I am against the shepherds. I will demand my flock from them and prevent them from shepherding the flock. The shepherds will no longer feed themselves, for I will rescue my flock from their mouths so that they will not be food for them.

11 "'For this is what the Lord GOD says: See, I myself will search for my flock and look for them. 12 As a shepherd looks for his sheep on the day he is among his scattered flock, so I will look for my flock. I will rescue them from all the places where they have been scattered on a day of clouds and total darkness. 13 I will bring them out from the peoples, gather them from the countries, and bring them to their own soil. I will shepherd them on the mountains of Israel, in the ravines, and in all the inhabited places of the land. 14 I will tend them in good pasture, and their grazing place will be on Israel's lofty mountains. There they will lie down in a good grazing place; they will feed in rich pasture on the mountains of Israel. 15 I will tend my flock and let them lie down. This is the declaration of the Lord GOD. 16 I will seek the lost, bring back the strays, bandage the injured, and strengthen the weak, but I will destroy the fat and the strong. I will shepherd them with justice.

17 "'As for you, my flock, the Lord GOD says this: Look, I am going to judge between one sheep and another, between the rams and goats. 18 Isn't it enough for you to feed on the good pasture? Must you also trample the rest of the pasture with your feet? Or isn't it enough that you drink the clear water? Must you also muddy the rest with your feet? 19 Yet my flock has to feed on what your feet have trampled, and drink what your feet have muddied.

20 "'Therefore, this is what the Lord GOD says to them: See, I myself will judge between the fat sheep and the lean sheep.

SHE READS TRUTH   DAY 30   147

21 Since you have pushed with flank and shoulder and butted all the weak ones with your horns until you scattered them all over, 22 I will save my flock. They will no longer be prey, and I will judge between one sheep and another. 23 I will establish over them one shepherd, my servant David, and he will shepherd them. He will tend them himself and will be their shepherd. 24 I, the Lord, will be their God, and my servant David will be a prince among them. I, the Lord, have spoken.

25 "'I will make a covenant of peace with them and eliminate dangerous creatures from the land, so that they may live securely in the wilderness and sleep in the forest. 26 I will make them and the area around my hill a blessing: I will send down showers in their season; they will be showers of blessing. 27 The trees of the field will yield their fruit, and the land will yield its produce; my flock will be secure in their land. They will know that I am the Lord when I break the bars of their yoke and rescue them from the power of those who enslave them. 28 They will no longer be prey for the nations, and the wild creatures of the earth will not consume them. They will live securely, and no one will frighten them. 29 I will establish for them a place renowned for its agriculture, and they will no longer be victims of famine in the land. They will no longer endure the insults of the nations. 30 Then they will know that I, the Lord their God, am with them, and that they, the house of Israel, are my people. This is the declaration of the Lord God. 31 You are my flock, the human flock of my pasture, and I am your God. This is the declaration of the Lord God.'"

EZEKIEL 35

A PROPHECY AGAINST EDOM

1 The word of the Lord came to me: 2 "Son of man, face Mount Seir and prophesy against it. 3 Say to it, 'This is what the Lord God says:

> Look! I am against you, Mount Seir.
> I will stretch out my hand against you
> and make you a desolate waste.
> 4 I will turn your cities into ruins,
> and you will become a desolation.
> Then you will know that I am the Lord.

5 "'Because you maintained a perpetual hatred and gave the Israelites over to the power of the sword in the time of their disaster, the time of final punishment, 6 therefore, as I live—this is the declaration of the Lord God—I will destine you for bloodshed, and it will pursue you. Since you did not hate bloodshed, it will pursue you. 7 I will make Mount Seir a desolate waste and will cut off from it those who come and go. 8 I will fill its mountains with the slain; those slain by the sword will fall on your hills, in your valleys, and in all your ravines. 9 I will make you a

perpetual desolation; your cities will not be inhabited. Then you will know that I am the LORD.

[10] "'Because you said, "These two nations and two lands will be mine, and we will possess them"—though the LORD was there— [11] therefore, as I live—this is the declaration of the Lord GOD—I will treat you according to the anger and jealousy you showed in your hatred of them. I will make myself known among them when I judge you. [12] Then you will know that I, the LORD, have heard all the blasphemies you uttered against the mountains of Israel, saying, "They are desolate. They have been given to us to devour!" [13] You boasted against me with your mouth, and spoke many words against me. I heard it myself!

[14] "'This is what the Lord GOD says: While the whole world rejoices, I will make you a desolation. [15] Just as you rejoiced over the inheritance of the house of Israel because it became a desolation, I will deal the same way with you: you will become a desolation, Mount Seir, and so will all Edom in its entirety. Then they will know that I am the LORD.'"

🔖 GOING DEEPER

PSALM 23:1-4

THE GOOD SHEPHERD

[1] The LORD is my shepherd;
I have what I need.
[2] He lets me lie down in green pastures;
he leads me beside quiet waters.
[3] He renews my life;
he leads me along the right paths
for his name's sake.
[4] Even when I go through the darkest valley,
I fear no danger,
for you are with me;
your rod and your staff—they comfort me.

JOHN 10:11-14

[11] "I am the good shepherd. The good shepherd lays down his life for the sheep. [12] The hired hand, since he is not the shepherd and doesn't own the sheep, leaves them and runs away when he sees a wolf coming. The wolf then snatches and scatters them. [13] This happens because he is a hired hand and doesn't care about the sheep.

[14] "I am the good shepherd. I know my own, and my own know me…"

The Valley of Dry Bones

DAY 31

EZEKIEL 36

RESTORATION OF ISRAEL'S MOUNTAINS

[1] "Son of man, prophesy to the mountains of Israel and say, 'Mountains of Israel, hear the word of the LORD. [2] This is what the Lord GOD says: Because the enemy has said about you, "Aha! The ancient heights have become our possession,"' [3] therefore, prophesy and say, 'This is what the Lord GOD says: Because they have made you desolate and have trampled you from every side, so that you became a possession for the rest of the nations and an object of people's gossip and slander, [4] therefore, mountains of Israel, hear the word of the Lord GOD. This is what the Lord GOD says to the mountains and hills, to the ravines and valleys, to the desolate ruins and abandoned cities, which have become plunder and a mockery to the rest of the nations all around.

[5] "'This is what the Lord GOD says: Certainly in my burning zeal I speak against the rest of the nations and all of Edom, who took my land as their own possession with wholehearted rejoicing and utter contempt so that its pastureland became plunder. [6] Therefore, prophesy concerning Israel's land, and say to the mountains and hills, to the ravines and valleys: This is what the Lord GOD says: Look, I speak in my burning zeal because you have endured the insults of the nations. [7] Therefore, this is what the Lord GOD says: I swear that the nations all around you will endure their own insults.

[8] "'You, mountains of Israel, will produce your branches and bear your fruit for my people Israel, since their arrival is near. [9] Look! I am on your side; I will turn toward you, and you will be tilled and sown. [10] I will fill you with people, with the whole house of Israel in its entirety. The cities will be inhabited and the ruins rebuilt. [11] I will fill you with people and animals, and they will increase and be fruitful. I will make you inhabited as you once were and make you better off than you were before. Then you will know that I am the LORD. [12] I will cause people, my people Israel, to walk on you; they will possess you, and you will be their inheritance. You will no longer deprive them of their children.

[13] "'This is what the Lord GOD says: Because some are saying to you, "You devour people and deprive your nation of children," [14] therefore, you will no longer devour people and deprive your nation of children. This is the declaration

of the Lord God. [15] I will no longer allow the insults of the nations to be heard against you, and you will not have to endure the reproach of the peoples anymore; you will no longer cause your nation to stumble. This is the declaration of the Lord God.'"

RESTORATION OF ISRAEL'S PEOPLE

[16] The word of the Lord came to me: [17] "Son of man, while the house of Israel lived in their land, they defiled it with their conduct and actions. Their behavior before me was like menstrual impurity. [18] So I poured out my wrath on them because of the blood they had shed on the land, and because they had defiled it with their idols. [19] I dispersed them among the nations, and they were scattered among the countries. I judged them according to their conduct and actions. [20] When they came to the nations where they went, they profaned my holy name, because it was said about them, 'These are the people of the Lord, yet they had to leave his land in exile.' [21] Then I had concern for my holy name, which the house of Israel profaned among the nations where they went.

[22] "Therefore, say to the house of Israel, 'This is what the Lord God says:

IT IS NOT FOR YOUR SAKE THAT I WILL ACT, HOUSE OF ISRAEL, BUT FOR MY HOLY NAME,

which you profaned among the nations where you went. [23] I will honor the holiness of my great name, which has been profaned among the nations—the name you have profaned among them. The nations will know that I am the Lord—this is the declaration of the Lord God—when I demonstrate my holiness through you in their sight.

[24] "'For I will take you from the nations and gather you from all the countries, and will bring you into your own land. [25] I will also sprinkle clean water on you, and you will be clean. I will cleanse you from all your impurities and all your idols. [26] I will give you a new heart and put a new spirit within you; I will remove your heart of stone and give you a heart of flesh. [27] I will place my Spirit within you and cause you to follow my statutes and carefully observe my ordinances.

[28] You will live in the land that I gave your ancestors; you will be my people, and I will be your God. [29] I will save you from all your uncleanness. I will summon the grain and make it plentiful, and I will not bring famine on you. [30] I will also make the fruit of the trees and the produce of the field plentiful, so that you will no longer experience reproach among the nations on account of famine.

[31] "'You will remember your evil ways and your deeds that were not good, and you will loathe yourselves for your iniquities and detestable practices. [32] It is not for your sake that I will act—this is the declaration of the Lord God—let this be known to you. Be ashamed and humiliated because of your ways, house of Israel!

[33] "'This is what the Lord God says: On the day I cleanse you from all your iniquities, I will cause the cities to be inhabited, and the ruins will be rebuilt. [34] The desolate land will be cultivated instead of lying desolate in the sight of everyone who passes by. [35] They will say, "This land that was desolate has become like the garden of Eden. The cities that were once ruined, desolate, and demolished are now fortified and inhabited." [36] Then the nations that remain around you will know that I, the Lord, have rebuilt what was demolished and have replanted what was desolate. I, the Lord, have spoken and I will do it.

[37] "'This is what the Lord God says: I will respond to the house of Israel and do this for them: I will multiply them in number like a flock. [38] So the ruined cities will be filled with a flock of people, just as Jerusalem is filled with a flock of sheep for sacrifice during its appointed festivals. Then they will know that I am the Lord.'"

EZEKIEL 37

THE VALLEY OF DRY BONES

[1] The hand of the Lord was on me, and he brought me out by his Spirit and set me down in the middle of the valley; it was full of bones. [2] He led me all around them. There were a great many of them on the surface of the valley, and they were very dry. [3] Then he said to me, "Son of man, can these bones live?"

I replied, "Lord God, only you know."

[4] He said to me, "Prophesy concerning these bones and say to them: Dry bones, hear the word of the Lord! [5] This is what the Lord God says to these bones: I will cause breath to enter you, and you will live. [6] I will put tendons on you, make flesh grow on you, and cover you with skin. I will put breath in you so that you come to life. Then you will know that I am the Lord."

[7] So I prophesied as I had been commanded. While I was prophesying, there was a noise, a rattling sound, and the bones came together, bone to bone. [8] As I looked, tendons appeared on them, flesh grew, and skin covered them, but there was no breath in them. [9] He said to me, "Prophesy to the breath, prophesy, son of man. Say to it: This is what the Lord God says: Breath, come from the four winds and breathe into these slain so that they may live!" [10] So I prophesied as he commanded me; the breath entered them, and they came to life and stood on their feet, a vast army.

[11] Then he said to me, "Son of man, these bones are the whole house of Israel. Look how they say, 'Our bones are dried up, and our hope has perished; we are cut off.' [12] Therefore, prophesy and say to them, 'This is what the Lord God says: I am going to open your graves and bring you up from them, my people, and lead you into the land of Israel. [13] You will know that I am the Lord, my people, when I open your graves and bring you up from them. [14] I will put my Spirit in you, and you will live, and I will settle you in your own land. Then you will know that I am the Lord. I have spoken, and I will do it. This is the declaration of the Lord.'"

THE REUNIFICATION OF ISRAEL

[15] The word of the Lord came to me: [16] "Son of man, take a single stick and write on it: Belonging to Judah and the Israelites associated with him. Then take another stick and write on it: Belonging to Joseph—the stick of Ephraim—and all the house of Israel associated with him. [17] Then join them together into a single stick so that they become one in your hand. [18] When your people ask you, 'Won't you explain to us what you mean by these things?'— [19] tell them, 'This is what the Lord God says: I am going to take the stick of Joseph, which is in the hand of Ephraim, and the tribes of Israel associated with him, and put them together with the stick of Judah. I will make them into a single stick so that they become one in my hand.'

[20] "When the sticks you have written on are in your hand and in full view of the people, [21] tell them, 'This is what the Lord God says: I am going to take the Israelites out of the nations where they have gone. I will gather them from all around and bring them into their own land. [22] I will make them one nation in the land, on the mountains of Israel, and one king will rule over all of them. They will no longer be two nations and will no longer be divided into two kingdoms. [23] They will not defile themselves anymore with their idols, their abhorrent things, and all

their transgressions. I will save them from all their apostasies by which they sinned, and I will cleanse them. Then they will be my people, and I will be their God. [24] My servant David will be king over them, and there will be one shepherd for all of them. They will follow my ordinances, and keep my statutes and obey them.

[25] "'They will live in the land that I gave to my servant Jacob, where your ancestors lived. They will live in it forever with their children and grandchildren, and my servant David will be their prince forever. [26] I will make a covenant of peace with them; it will be a permanent covenant with them. I will establish and multiply them and will set my sanctuary among them forever. [27] My dwelling place will be with them; I will be their God, and they will be my people. [28] When my sanctuary is among them forever, the nations will know that I, the LORD, sanctify Israel.'"

◗ GOING DEEPER

HOSEA 6:1-3

A CALL TO REPENTANCE

[1] Come, let's return to the LORD.
For he has torn us,
and he will heal us;
he has wounded us,
and he will bind up our wounds.
[2] He will revive us after two days,
and on the third day he will raise us up
so we can live in his presence.
[3] Let's strive to know the LORD.
His appearance is as sure as the dawn.
He will come to us like the rain,
like the spring showers that water the land.

JOHN 11:23-26

[23] "Your brother will rise again," Jesus told her.

[24] Martha said to him, "I know that he will rise again in the resurrection at the last day."

[25] Jesus said to her, "I am the resurrection and the life. The one who believes in me, even if he dies, will live. [26] Everyone who lives and believes in me will never die. Do you believe this?"

"Look! I am on your side;

I will turn toward you."

EZEKIEL 36:9

Israel's Restoration to God

32

EZEKIEL 38

THE DEFEAT OF GOG

¹ The word of the LORD came to me: ² "Son of man, face Gog, of the land of Magog, the chief prince of Meshech and Tubal. Prophesy against him ³ and say, 'This is what the Lord GOD says: Look, I am against you, Gog, chief prince of Meshech and Tubal. ⁴ I will turn you around, put hooks in your jaws, and bring you out with all your army, including horses and riders, who are all splendidly dressed, a huge assembly armed with large and small shields, all of them brandishing swords. ⁵ Persia, Cush, and Put are with them, all of them with shields and helmets; ⁶ Gomer with all its troops; and Beth-togarmah from the remotest parts of the north along with all its troops—many peoples are with you.

⁷ "'Be prepared and get yourself ready, you and your whole assembly that has been mobilized around you; you will be their guard. ⁸ After a long time you will be summoned. In the last years you will enter a land that has been restored from war and regathered from many peoples to the mountains of Israel, which had long been a ruin. They were brought out from the peoples, and all of them now live securely. ⁹ You, all of your troops, and many peoples with you will advance, coming like a thunderstorm; you will be like a cloud covering the land.

¹⁰ "'This is what the Lord GOD says: On that day, thoughts will arise in your mind, and you will devise an evil plan. ¹¹ You will say, "I will advance against a land of open villages; I will come against a tranquil people who are living securely, all of them living without walls and without bars or gates"— ¹² in order to seize spoil and carry off plunder, to turn your hand against ruins now inhabited and against a people gathered from the nations, who have been acquiring cattle and possessions and who live at the center of the world. ¹³ Sheba and Dedan and the merchants of Tarshish with all its rulers will ask you, "Have you come to seize spoil? Have you mobilized your assembly to carry off plunder, to make off with silver and gold, to take cattle and possessions, to seize plenty of spoil?"'

¹⁴ "Therefore prophesy, son of man, and say to Gog, 'This is what the Lord GOD says: On that day when my people Israel are dwelling securely, will you not know this ¹⁵ and come from your place in the remotest parts of the north—you and many peoples with you, who are all riding horses—a huge assembly, a powerful army? ¹⁶ You will advance against my people Israel like a cloud covering the land. It will happen in the last days, Gog, that I will bring you against my land so that the nations may know me, when I demonstrate my holiness through you in their sight.

¹⁷ "'This is what the Lord GOD says: Are you the one I spoke about in former times through my servants, the prophets of Israel, who for years prophesied in those times that I would bring you against them? ¹⁸ Now on that day, the day when Gog comes against the land of Israel—this is the declaration of the Lord GOD—my wrath will flare up. ¹⁹ I swear in my zeal and fiery wrath: On that day there will be a great earthquake in the land of Israel. ²⁰ The fish of the sea, the birds of the sky, the animals of the field, every creature that crawls on the ground, and every human being on the face of the earth will tremble before me. The mountains will be demolished, the cliffs will collapse, and every wall will fall to the ground. ²¹ I will call for a sword against him on all my mountains—this is the declaration of the Lord GOD—and every man's sword will be against his brother. ²² I will execute judgment on him with plague and bloodshed. I will pour out torrential rain, hailstones, fire, and burning sulfur on him, as well as his troops and the many peoples who are with him. ²³ I will display my greatness and holiness, and will reveal myself in the sight of many nations. Then they will know that I am the LORD.'"

EZEKIEL 39

THE DISPOSAL OF GOG

¹ "As for you, son of man, prophesy against Gog and say, 'This is what the Lord GOD says: Look, I am against you, Gog, chief prince of Meshech and Tubal. ² I will turn you around, drive you on, and lead you up from the remotest parts of the north. I will bring you against the mountains of Israel. ³ Then I will knock your bow from your left hand and make your arrows drop from your right hand. ⁴ You, all your troops, and the peoples who are with you will fall on the mountains of Israel. I will give you as food to every kind of

predatory bird and to the wild animals. [5] You will fall on the open field, for I have spoken. This is the declaration of the Lord GOD.

[6] "'I will send fire against Magog and those who live securely on the coasts and islands. Then they will know that I am the LORD. [7] So I will make my holy name known among my people Israel and will no longer allow it to be profaned. Then the nations will know that I am the LORD, the Holy One in Israel. [8] Yes, it is coming, and it will happen. This is the declaration of the Lord GOD. This is the day I have spoken about.

[9] "'Then the inhabitants of Israel's cities will go out, kindle fires, and burn the weapons—the small and large shields, the bows and arrows, the clubs and spears. For seven years they will use them to make fires. [10] They will not gather wood from the countryside or cut it down from the forests, for they will use the weapons to make fires. They will take the loot from those who looted them and plunder those who plundered them. This is the declaration of the Lord GOD.

[11] "'Now on that day I will give Gog a burial place there in Israel—the Travelers' Valley east of the Sea. It will block those who travel through, for Gog and all his hordes will be buried there. So it will be called Hordes of Gog Valley. [12] The house of Israel will spend seven months burying them in order to cleanse the land. [13] All the people of the land will bury them and their fame will spread on the day I display my glory. This is the declaration of the Lord GOD.

[14] "'They will appoint men on a full-time basis to pass through the land and bury the invaders who remain on the surface of the ground, in order to cleanse it. They will make their search at the end of the seven months. [15] When they pass through the land and one of them sees a human bone, he will set up a marker next to it until the buriers have buried it in Hordes of Gog Valley. [16] There will even be a city named Hamonah there. So they will cleanse the land.'

[17] "Son of man, this is what the Lord GOD says: Tell every kind of bird and all the wild animals, 'Assemble and come! Gather from all around to my sacrificial feast that I am slaughtering for you, a great feast on the mountains of Israel; you will eat flesh and drink blood. [18] You will eat the flesh of mighty men and drink the blood of the earth's princes: rams, lambs, male goats, and all the fattened bulls of Bashan. [19] You will eat fat until you are satisfied and drink blood until you are drunk, at my sacrificial feast that I have prepared for you. [20] At my table you will eat your fill of horses and riders, of mighty men and all the warriors. This is the declaration of the Lord GOD.'

ISRAEL'S RESTORATION TO GOD

[21] "I will display my glory among the nations, and all the nations will see the judgment I have executed and the hand I have laid on them. [22] From that day

forward the house of Israel will know that I am the LORD their God. [23] And the nations will know that the house of Israel went into exile on account of their iniquity, because they dealt unfaithfully with me. Therefore, I hid my face from them and handed them over to their enemies, so that they all fell by the sword. [24] I dealt with them according to their uncleanness and transgressions, and I hid my face from them.

[25] "So this is what the Lord GOD says: Now I will restore the fortunes of Jacob and have compassion on the whole house of Israel, and I will be jealous for my holy name. [26] They will feel remorse for their disgrace and all the unfaithfulness they committed against me, when they live securely in their land with no one to frighten them. [27] When I bring them back from the peoples and gather them from the countries of their enemies, I will demonstrate my holiness through them in the sight of many nations. [28] They will know that I am the LORD their God when I regather them to their own land after having exiled them among the nations. I will leave none of them behind. [29] I will no longer hide my face from them, for I will pour out my Spirit on the house of Israel." This is the declaration of the Lord GOD.

🔖 GOING DEEPER

PSALM 107:1–3

THANKSGIVING FOR GOD'S DELIVERANCE

[1] Give thanks to the LORD, for he is good;
his faithful love endures forever.
[2] Let the redeemed of the LORD proclaim
that he has redeemed them from the power of the foe
[3] and has gathered them from the lands—
from the east and the west,
from the north and the south.

The New Temple

EZEKIEL 40

THE NEW TEMPLE

¹ In the twenty-fifth year of our exile, at the beginning of the year, on the tenth day of the month in the fourteenth year after Jerusalem had been captured, on that very day the LORD's hand was on me, and he brought me there. ² In visions of God he took me to the land of Israel and set me down on a very high mountain. On its southern slope was a structure resembling a city. ³ He brought me there, and I saw a man whose appearance was like bronze, with a linen cord and a measuring rod in his hand. He was standing by the city gate. ⁴ He spoke to me: "Son of man, look with your eyes, listen with your ears, and pay attention to everything I am going to show you, for you have been brought here so that I might show it to you. Report everything you see to the house of Israel."

THE WALL AND OUTER GATES

⁵ Now there was a wall surrounding the outside of the temple. The measuring rod in the man's hand was six units of twenty-one inches; each unit was the standard length plus three inches. He measured the thickness of the wall structure; it was 10½ feet, and its height was the same. ⁶ Then he came to the gate that faced east and climbed its steps. He measured the threshold of the gate; it was 10½ feet deep—one threshold was 10½ feet deep. ⁷ Each recess was 10½ feet long and 10½ feet deep, and there was a space of 8¾ feet between the recesses. The inner threshold of the gate on the temple side next to the gate's portico was 10½ feet. ⁸ Next he measured the gate's portico; ⁹ it was 14 feet, and its jambs were 3½ feet. The gate's portico was on the temple side.

¹⁰ There were three recesses on each side of the east gate, each with the same measurements, and the jambs on either side also had the same measurements. ¹¹ Then he measured the width of the gate's entrance; it was 17½ feet, while the width of the gate was 22¾ feet. ¹² There was a barrier of 21 inches in front of the recesses on both sides, and the recesses on each side were 10½ feet square. ¹³ Then he measured the gate from the roof of one recess to the roof of the opposite one; the distance was 43¾ feet. The openings of the recesses faced each other. ¹⁴ Next, he measured the porch—105 feet. ¹⁵ The distance from the front of the gate at the entrance to the front of the gate's portico on the inside was 87½ feet. ¹⁶ The recesses and their jambs had beveled windows all around the inside of the gate. The porticoes also had windows all around on the inside. Each jamb was decorated with palm trees.

¹⁷ Then he brought me into the outer court, and there were chambers and a paved surface laid out all around the court. Thirty chambers faced the pavement, ¹⁸ which flanked the courtyard's gates and corresponded to the length of the gates; this was the lower pavement. ¹⁹ Then he measured the distance from the front of the lower gate to the exterior front of the inner court; it was 175 feet. This was the east; next the north is described.

[20] He measured the gate of the outer court facing north, both its length and width. [21] Its three recesses on each side, its jambs, and its portico had the same measurements as the first gate: 87½ feet long and 43¾ feet wide. [22] Its windows, portico, and palm trees had the same measurements as those of the gate that faced east. Seven steps led up to the gate, and its portico was ahead of them. [23] The inner court had a gate facing the north gate, like the one on the east. He measured the distance from gate to gate; it was 175 feet.

[24] He brought me to the south side, and there was also a gate on the south. He measured its jambs and portico; they had the same measurements as the others. [25] Both the gate and its portico had windows all around, like the other windows. It was 87½ feet long and 43¾ feet wide. [26] Its stairway had seven steps, and its portico was ahead of them. It had palm trees on its jambs, one on each side. [27] The inner court had a gate on the south. He measured from gate to gate on the south; it was 175 feet.

THE INNER GATES

[28] Then he brought me to the inner court through the south gate. When he measured the south gate, it had the same measurements as the others. [29] Its recesses, jambs, and portico had the same measurements as the others. Both it and its portico had windows all around. It was 87½ feet long and 43¾ feet wide. [30] (There were porticoes all around, 43¾ feet long and 8¾ feet wide.) [31] Its portico faced the outer court, and its jambs were decorated with palm trees. Its stairway had eight steps.

[32] Then he brought me to the inner court on the east side. When he measured the gate, it had the same measurements as the others. [33] Its recesses, jambs, and portico had the same measurements as the others. Both it and its portico had windows all around. It was 87½ feet long and 43¾ feet wide. [34] Its portico faced the outer court, and its jambs were decorated with palm trees on each side. Its stairway had eight steps.

[35] Then he brought me to the north gate. When he measured it, it had the same measurements as the others, [36] as did its recesses, jambs, and portico. It also had windows all around. It was 87½ feet long and 43¾ feet wide. [37] Its portico faced the outer court, and its jambs were decorated with palm trees on each side. Its stairway had eight steps.

ROOMS FOR PREPARING SACRIFICES

[38] There was a chamber whose door opened into the gate's portico. The burnt offering was to be washed there. [39] Inside the gate's portico there were two tables on each side, on which to slaughter the burnt offering, sin offering, and guilt offering. [40] Outside, as one approaches the entrance of the north gate, there were two tables on one side and two more tables on the other side of the gate's portico. [41] So there

were four tables inside the gate and four outside, eight tables in all on which the slaughtering was to be done. ⁴² There were also four tables of cut stone for the burnt offering, each 31½ inches long, 31½ inches wide, and 21 inches high. The utensils used to slaughter the burnt offerings and other sacrifices were placed on them. ⁴³ There were three-inch hooks fastened all around the inside of the room, and the flesh of the offering was to be laid on the tables.

ROOMS FOR SINGERS AND PRIESTS

⁴⁴ Outside the inner gate, within the inner court, there were chambers for the singers: one beside the north gate, facing south, and another beside the south gate, facing north. ⁴⁵ Then the man said to me, "This chamber that faces south is for the priests who keep charge of the temple. ⁴⁶ The chamber that faces north is for the priests who keep charge of the altar. These are the sons of Zadok, the ones from the sons of Levi who may approach the LORD to serve him." ⁴⁷ Next he measured the court. It was square, 175 feet long and 175 feet wide. The altar was in front of the temple.

⁴⁸ Then he brought me to the portico of the temple and measured the jambs of the portico; they were 8¾ feet thick on each side. The width of the gate was 24½ feet, and the side walls of the gate were 5¼ feet wide on each side. ⁴⁹ The portico was 35 feet across and 21 feet deep, and 10 steps led up to it. There were pillars by the jambs, one on each side.

EZEKIEL 41:1–4

INSIDE THE TEMPLE

¹ Next he brought me into the great hall and measured the jambs; on each side the width of the jamb was 10½ feet. ² The width of the entrance was 17½ feet, and the side walls of the entrance were 8¾ feet wide on each side. He also measured the length of the great hall, 70 feet, and the width, 35 feet. ³ He went inside the next room and measured the jambs at the entrance; they were 3½ feet wide. The entrance was 10½ feet wide, and the width of the entrance's side walls on each side was 12¼ feet. ⁴ He then measured the length of the room adjacent to the great hall, 35 feet, and the width, 35 feet. And he said to me, "This is the most holy place."

🔖 GOING DEEPER

JOHN 1:14–16

¹⁴ The Word became flesh and dwelt among us. We observed his glory, the glory as the one and only Son from the Father, full of grace and truth. ¹⁵ (John testified concerning him and exclaimed, "This was the one of whom I said, 'The one coming after me ranks ahead of me, because he existed before me.'") ¹⁶ Indeed, we have all received grace upon grace from his fullness…

JOHN 2:13–22

CLEANSING THE TEMPLE

¹³ The Jewish Passover was near, and so Jesus went up to Jerusalem. ¹⁴ In the temple he found people selling oxen, sheep, and doves, and he also found the money changers sitting there. ¹⁵ After making a whip out of cords, he drove everyone out of the temple with their sheep and oxen. He also poured out the money changers' coins and overturned the tables. ¹⁶ He told those who were selling doves, "Get these things out of here! Stop turning my Father's house into a marketplace!"

¹⁷ And his disciples remembered that it is written: Zeal for your house will consume me.

¹⁸ So the Jews replied to him, "What sign will you show us for doing these things?"

¹⁹ Jesus answered, "Destroy this temple, and I will raise it up in three days."

²⁰ Therefore the Jews said, "This temple took forty-six years to build, and will you raise it up in three days?"

²¹ But he was speaking about the temple of his body. ²² So when he was raised from the dead, his disciples remembered that he had said this, and they believed the Scripture and the statement Jesus had made.

Notes

Response

LAMENT

During this Lenten season, we make time to lament— to grieve our own sin and express sorrow over the brokenness of the world, to which our sin contributes.

1 What in your life do you need to lament? Take time to confess your own sin and grieve over how the sin of others has affected you.

2 How does your sin and brokenness affect your community? Take time to lament for the brokenness you see in the world.

CONFESSION
AND ASSURANCE

A lament is not a quick
fix, but God is faithful,
and lamenting gently but
persistently reminds us to
trust Him. Use this space to
confess your need for God
and His intervention, as well
as express your continued
hope found in His provision.

Softly and Tenderly

WORDS
Will L. Thompson

MUSIC
Will L. Thompson

1. Soft - ly and ten - der - ly Je - sus is call - ing, Call-ing for you and for me;
2. Why should we tar - ry when Je - sus is plead-ing, Plead ing for you and for me?
3. Time is now fleet-ing, the mo - ments are pass - ing, Pass-ing from you and from me;
4. Oh! for the won-der-ful love He has prom-ised, Prom-ised for you and for me;

See, on the por - tals He's wait-ing and watch-ing, Watch-ing for you and for me.
Why should we lin - ger and heed not His mer - cies, Mer-cies for you and for me?
Shad - ows are gath - er-ing, death-beds are com - ing, Com ing for you and for me.
Though we have sinned He has mer - cy and par - don, Par don for you and for me.

Chorus

Come home, come home, Ye who are wea-ry come home;

Come home, come home,

Ear-nest-ly, ten-der-ly, Je-sus is call-ing, Call-ing, O sin-ner, come home!

Rebecca Hunter, *Ambrose,* 2020, house paint, copper wire, and paper on canvas, 30x40 in.

GRACE DAY

Come, let's return to the LORD.
For he has torn us, and he will
heal us; he has wounded us, and
he will bind up our wounds.

HOSEA 6:1

DAY 34

Lent is a season where we reflect on the depth of our sin and embrace the hope and strength found only in the cross of Christ. We seek unhurried moments of quiet to read Scripture, pray, confess, and repent. Take some time today to catch up on your reading, make space for prayer, and rest in God's presence.

35

Weekly Truth

Scripture is God-breathed and true. When we memorize it, we carry His Word with us wherever we go.

Over the last six weeks, we have memorized Ezekiel 36:26–28. Spend some time reviewing the full passage to strengthen your memorization. Let these words remind you of this: those who are in Christ are His, and nothing can change that.

"I will give you a new heart and put a new spirit within you; I will remove your heart of stone and give you a heart of flesh. I will place my Spirit within you and cause you to follow my statutes and carefully observe my ordinances. You will live in the land that I gave your ancestors; you will be my people, and I will be your God."

EZEKIEL 36:26–28

See tips for memorizing Scripture on page 236.

The Return of the Lord's Glory

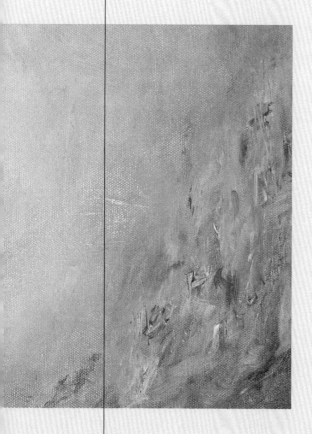

EZEKIEL 41:5-26

OUTSIDE THE TEMPLE

[5] Then he measured the wall of the temple; it was 10½ feet thick. The width of the side rooms all around the temple was 7 feet. [6] The side rooms were arranged one above another in three stories of thirty rooms each. There were ledges on the wall of the temple all around to serve as supports for the side rooms, so that the supports would not be in the temple wall itself. [7] The side rooms surrounding the temple widened at each successive story, for the structure surrounding the temple went up by stages. This was the reason for the temple's broadness as it rose. And so, one would go up from the lowest story to the highest by means of the middle one.

[8] I saw that the temple had a raised platform surrounding it; this foundation for the side rooms was 10½ feet high. [9] The thickness of the outer wall of the side rooms was 8¾ feet. The free space between the side rooms of the temple [10] and the outer chambers was 35 feet wide all around the temple. [11] The side rooms opened into the free space, one entrance toward the north and another to the south. The area of free space was 8¾ feet wide all around.

[12] Now the building that faced the temple yard toward the west was 122½ feet wide. The wall of the building was 8¾ feet thick on all sides, and the building's length was 157½ feet.

[13] Then the man measured the temple; it was 175 feet long. In addition, the temple yard and the building, including its walls, were 175 feet long. [14] The width of the front of the temple along with the temple yard to the east was 175 feet. [15] Next he measured the length of the building facing the temple yard to the west, with its galleries on each side; it was 175 feet.

INTERIOR WOODEN STRUCTURES

The interior of the great hall and the porticoes of the court— [16] the thresholds, the beveled windows, and the balconies all around with their three levels opposite the threshold—were overlaid with wood on all sides. They were paneled from the ground to the windows (but the windows were covered), [17] reaching to the top of the entrance, and as far as the inner temple and on the outside. On every wall all around, on the inside and outside, was a pattern [18] carved with cherubim and palm trees. There was a palm tree between each pair of cherubim. Each cherub had two faces: [19] a human face turned toward the palm tree on one side, and a lion's face turned toward it on the other. They were carved throughout the temple on all sides. [20] Cherubim and palm trees were carved from the ground to the top of the entrance and on the wall of the great hall.

[21] The doorposts of the great hall were square, and the front of the sanctuary had the same appearance. [22] The altar was made of wood, 5¼ feet high and 3½ feet long. It had corners, and its length and sides were of wood. The man told me, "This is the table that stands before the LORD."

[23] The great hall and the sanctuary each had a double door, [24] and each of the doors had two swinging panels. There were two panels for one door and two for the other. [25] Cherubim and palm trees were carved on the doors of the great hall like those carved on the walls. There was a wooden canopy outside, in front of the portico. [26] There were beveled windows and palm trees on both sides, on the side walls of the portico, the side rooms of the temple, and the canopies.

EZEKIEL 42

THE PRIESTS' CHAMBERS

[1] Then the man led me out by way of the north gate into the outer court. He brought me to the group of chambers opposite the temple yard and opposite the building to the north. [2] Along the length of the chambers, which was 175 feet, there was an entrance on the north; the width was 87½ feet. [3] Opposite the 35 foot space belonging to the inner court and opposite the paved surface belonging to the outer court, the structure rose gallery by gallery in three tiers. [4] In front of the chambers was a walkway toward the inside, 17½ feet wide and 175 feet long, and their entrances were on the north. [5] The upper chambers were narrower because the galleries took away more space from them than from the lower and middle stories of the building. [6] For they were arranged in three stories and had no pillars like the pillars of the courts; therefore the upper chambers were set back from the ground more than the lower and middle stories. [7] A wall on the outside ran in front of the chambers, parallel to them, toward the outer court; it was 87½ feet long. [8] For the chambers on the outer court were 87½ feet long, while those facing the great hall were 175 feet long. [9] At the base of these chambers there was an entryway on the east side as one enters them from the outer court.

[10] In the thickness of the wall of the court toward the south, there were chambers facing the temple yard and the western building, [11] with a passageway in front of them, just like the chambers that faced north. Their length and width, as well as all their exits, measurements, and entrances, were identical. [12] The entrance at the beginning of the passageway, the way in front of the corresponding wall as one enters on the east side, was similar to the entrances of the chambers that were on the south side.

13 Then the man said to me, "The northern and southern chambers that face the courtyard are the holy chambers where the priests who approach the LORD will eat the most holy offerings. There they will deposit the most holy offerings— the grain offerings, sin offerings, and guilt offerings—for the place is holy. 14 Once the priests have entered, they are not to go out from the holy area to the outer court until they have removed the clothes they minister in, for these are holy. They are to put on other clothes before they approach the public area."

OUTSIDE DIMENSIONS OF THE TEMPLE COMPLEX

15 When he finished measuring inside the temple complex, he led me out by way of the gate that faced east and measured all around the complex.

16 He measured the east side with a measuring rod;
it was 875 feet by the measuring rod.
17 He measured the north side;
it was 875 feet by the measuring rod.
18 He measured the south side;
it was 875 feet by the measuring rod.
19 Then he turned to the west side
and measured 875 feet by the measuring rod.

20 He measured the temple complex on all four sides. It had a wall all around it, 875 feet long and 875 feet wide, to separate the holy from the common.

EZEKIEL 43:1-12

THE RETURN OF THE LORD'S GLORY

1 He led me to the gate, the one that faces east, 2 and I saw the glory of the God of Israel coming from the east. His voice sounded like the roar of a huge torrent, and the earth shone with his glory. 3 The vision I saw was like the one I had seen when he came to destroy the city, and like the ones I had seen by the Chebar Canal. I fell facedown. 4 The glory of the LORD entered the temple by way of the gate that faced east. 5 Then the Spirit lifted me up and brought me to the inner court, and the glory of the LORD filled the temple.

6 While the man was standing beside me, I heard someone speaking to me from the temple. 7 He said to me, "Son of man, this is the place of my throne and the place for the soles of my feet, where I will dwell among the Israelites forever. The house of Israel and their kings will no longer defile my holy name by their religious prostitution and by the corpses of their kings at their high places. 8 Whenever they placed their threshold next to my threshold and their doorposts beside my doorposts, with only a wall between me and them, they were defiling my holy name by the detestable acts they committed. So I destroyed them in my anger. 9 Now let them remove their prostitution and the corpses of their kings far from me, and I will dwell among them forever.

10 "As for you, son of man, describe the temple to the house of Israel, so that they may be ashamed of their iniquities. Let them measure its pattern, 11 and they will be ashamed of all that they have done. Reveal the design of the temple to them—its layout with its exits and entrances—its complete design along with all its statutes, design specifications, and laws. Write it down in their sight so that they may observe its complete design and all its statutes and may carry them out. 12 This is the law of the temple: All its surrounding territory on top of the mountain will be especially holy. Yes, this is the law of the temple."

🔖 GOING DEEPER

1 CORINTHIANS 3:16-17

16 Don't you yourselves know that you are God's temple and that the Spirit of God lives in you? 17 If anyone destroys God's temple, God will destroy him; for God's temple is holy, and that is what you are.

EPHESIANS 2:19-22

19 So, then, you are no longer foreigners and strangers, but fellow citizens with the saints, and members of God's household, 20 built on the foundation of the apostles and prophets, with Christ Jesus himself as the cornerstone. 21 In him the whole building, being put together, grows into a holy temple in the Lord. 22 In him you are also being built together for God's dwelling in the Spirit.

Notes

The Priests' Duties and Privileges

37

THE ALTAR

¹³ "These are the measurements of the altar in units of length (each unit being the standard length plus three inches): The gutter is 21 inches deep and 21 inches wide, with a rim of nine inches around its edge. This is the base of the altar. ¹⁴ The distance from the gutter on the ground to the lower ledge is 3½ feet, and the width of the ledge is 21 inches. There are 7 feet from the small ledge to the large ledge, whose width is also 21 inches. ¹⁵ The altar hearth is 7 feet high, and four horns project upward from the hearth. ¹⁶ The hearth is square, 21 feet long by 21 feet wide. ¹⁷ The ledge is 24½ feet long by 24½ feet wide, with four equal sides. The rim all around it is 10½ inches, and its gutter is 21 inches all around it. The altar's steps face east."

¹⁸ Then he said to me, "Son of man, this is what the Lord God says: These are the statutes for the altar on the day it is constructed, so that burnt offerings may be sacrificed on it and blood may be splattered on it: ¹⁹ You are to give a bull from the herd as a sin offering to the Levitical priests who are from the offspring of Zadok, who approach me in order to serve me." This is the declaration of the Lord God. ²⁰ "You are to take some of its blood and apply it to the four horns of the altar, the four corners of the ledge, and all around the rim. In this way you will purify the altar and make atonement for it. ²¹ Then you are to take away the bull for the sin offering, and it must be burned outside the sanctuary in the place appointed for the temple.

²² "On the second day you are to present an unblemished male goat as a sin offering. They will purify the altar just as they did with the bull. ²³ When you have finished the purification, you are to present a young, unblemished bull and an unblemished ram from the flock. ²⁴ You are to present them before the Lord; the priests will throw salt on them and sacrifice them as a burnt offering to the Lord. ²⁵ You will offer a goat for a sin offering each day for seven days. A young bull and a ram from the flock, both unblemished, are also to be offered. ²⁶ For seven days the priests are to make atonement for the altar and cleanse it. In this way they will consecrate it ²⁷ and complete the days of purification. Then on the eighth day and afterward, the priests will offer your burnt offerings and fellowship offerings on the altar, and I will accept you." This is the declaration of the Lord God.

EZEKIEL 44

THE PRINCE'S PRIVILEGE

¹ The man then brought me back toward the sanctuary's outer gate that faced east, and it was closed. ² The Lord said to me, "This gate will remain closed. It will not be opened, and no one will enter through it, because the Lord, the God of Israel, has entered through it. Therefore it will remain closed. ³ The prince himself will sit in the gate to eat a meal before the Lord. He is to enter by way of the portico of the gate and go out the same way."

⁴ Then the man brought me by way of the north gate to the front of the temple. I looked, and the glory of the Lord filled his temple. And I fell facedown. ⁵ The Lord said to me, "Son of man, pay attention; look with your eyes and listen with your ears to everything I tell you about all the statutes and laws of the Lord's temple. Take careful note of the entrance of the temple along with all the exits of the sanctuary.

THE LEVITES' DUTIES AND PRIVILEGES

⁶ "Say to the rebellious people, the house of Israel, 'This is what the Lord God says: I have had enough of all your detestable practices, house of Israel. ⁷ When you brought in foreigners, uncircumcised in both heart and flesh, to occupy my sanctuary, you defiled my temple while you offered my food—the fat and the blood. You broke my covenant by all your detestable practices. ⁸ You have not kept charge of my holy things but have appointed others to keep charge of my sanctuary for you.'

⁹ "This is what the Lord God says: No foreigner, uncircumcised in heart and flesh, may enter my sanctuary, not even a foreigner who is among the Israelites. ¹⁰ Surely the Levites who wandered away from me when Israel went astray, and who strayed from me after their idols, will bear the consequences of their iniquity. ¹¹ Yet they will occupy

my sanctuary, serving as guards at the temple gates and ministering at the temple. They will slaughter the burnt offerings and other sacrifices for the people and will stand before them to serve them. [12] Because they ministered to the house of Israel before their idols and became a sinful stumbling block to them, therefore I swore an oath against them"—this is the declaration of the Lord GOD—"that they would bear the consequences of their iniquity. [13] They must not approach me to serve me as priests or come near any of my holy things or the most holy things. They will bear their disgrace and the consequences of the detestable acts they committed. [14] Yet I will make them responsible for the duties of the temple—for all its work and everything done in it.

THE PRIESTS' DUTIES AND PRIVILEGES

[15] "But the Levitical priests descended from Zadok, who kept charge of my sanctuary when the Israelites went astray from me, will approach me to serve me. They will stand before me to offer me fat and blood." This is the declaration of the Lord GOD. [16] "They are the ones who may enter my sanctuary and approach my table to serve me. They will keep my mandate. [17] When they enter the gates of the inner court they are to wear linen garments; they must not have on them anything made of wool when they minister at the gates of the inner court and within it. [18] They are to wear linen turbans on their heads and linen undergarments around their waists. They are not to put on anything that makes them sweat. [19] Before they go out to the outer court, to the people, they must take off the clothes they have been ministering in, leave them in the holy chambers, and dress in other clothes so that they do not transmit holiness to the people through their clothes.

[20] "They may not shave their heads or let their hair grow long, but are to carefully trim their hair. [21] No priest may drink wine before he enters the inner court. [22] He is not to marry a widow or a divorced woman, but may marry only a virgin from the offspring of the house of Israel, or a widow who is the widow of a priest. [23] They are to teach my people the difference between the holy and the common, and explain to them the difference between the clean and the unclean.

[24] "In a dispute, they will officiate as judges and decide the case according to my ordinances. They are to observe my laws and statutes regarding all my appointed festivals, and keep my Sabbaths holy. [25] A priest may not come near a dead person so that he becomes defiled. However, he may defile himself for a father, a mother, a son, a daughter, a brother, or an unmarried sister. [26] After he is cleansed, he is to count off seven days for himself. [27] On the day he goes into the sanctuary, into the inner court to minister in the sanctuary, he is to present his sin offering." This is the declaration of the Lord GOD.

[28] "This will be their inheritance: I am their inheritance. You are to give them no possession in Israel: I am their possession. [29] They will eat the grain offering, the sin offering, and the guilt offering. Everything in Israel that is permanently dedicated to the LORD will belong to them. [30] The best of all the firstfruits of every kind and contribution of every kind from all your gifts will belong to the priests. You are to give your first batch of dough to the priest so that a blessing may rest on your homes. [31] The priests may not eat any bird or animal that died naturally or was mauled by wild beasts."

♥ GOING DEEPER

1 PETER 2:9

But you are a chosen race, a royal priesthood, a holy nation, a people for his possession, so that you may proclaim the praises of the one who called you out of darkness into his marvelous light.

REVELATION 5:10

You made them a kingdom
and priests to our God,
and they will reign on the earth.

Notes

The Temple in Scripture

One key theme in the book of Ezekiel is the prophet's vision of the temple in Jerusalem and of a new temple in the future. Throughout Scripture, specific spaces and buildings were designated as meeting places for God and His people.

From the garden of Eden to the new heavens and the new earth, temples play an essential role in understanding God's presence. Here is a look at how God dwells among His people in unique ways throughout redemption history. Notice where Ezekiel's prophetic ministry takes place, including his prophecies about the new temple and the return of God's presence.

THE GARDEN OF EDEN

At creation, Adam and Eve—the first humans—enjoyed God's presence in the midst of a garden paradise called Eden. No temple structure was needed because they had direct access to God. However, their disobedience resulted in their expulsion from the garden and from God's presence.

THE TABERNACLE

Although humanity was separated from God's presence because of sin, God still planned to dwell among His people. During Israel's days of wandering in the wilderness, God instructed Moses to create a sacred space for worship—the tabernacle. This mobile sanctuary, resembling a large tent, featured furnishings crafted with the finest materials made to exact specifications to reflect God's holiness. Because it was set apart for God's glorious presence, the tabernacle was to be kept free of physical and spiritual contamination.

THE FIRST TEMPLE

King David's son, Solomon, built the first temple in Jerusalem, fulfilling David's desire to build a permanent structure for God's presence to dwell. Even with a temple to enter and access God's presence, God's people rebelled against His laws and worshiped idols. In a vision, Ezekiel saw God's presence and glory depart from the temple in Jerusalem as a judgment on the people's idolatry and disregard for worship (Ezk 10).

As judgment for their repeated disobedience, God issued prophetic warnings that foretold the exile of His people and the destruction of the temple itself. This came to pass after generations of disobedience, when Nebuchadnezzar laid siege to Jerusalem in 586 BC, destroying the city and the temple.

THE SECOND TEMPLE

Beginning in 538 BC, King Cyrus allowed exiles from Judah to return to Jerusalem and begin rebuilding the temple. Under the leadership of Zerubbabel and the prophets Haggai and Zechariah, the second temple was completed. Years later, Herod Agrippa I remodeled and expanded the temple. This is the same temple prominent in the Gospel narratives. The temple was destroyed in AD 70 by the Roman general Titus.

JESUS

Jesus, the Son of God, came to earth during the Second Temple period. The four Gospels announce that Jesus's life, death, and resurrection are the fulfillment of God's promise to send a new King and Savior who would restore what was lost in the garden. Fulfilling His mission on earth, Jesus removed the need for a temple to access God, declaring Himself to be the true temple (Jn 2:18–21).

THE CHURCH

With His life, death, and resurrection, Jesus established a new covenant. Those who follow Him are grafted into the people of God. Filled with the Holy Spirit, believers are the new temple, the dwelling place of Jesus's presence. While the Church still often gathers in buildings today, a physical space is no longer needed for believers to access the presence of God. Jesus has commissioned believers— His living temples—to carry His life-changing presence to the world.

THE HOLY CITY

One day, the whole earth will be made new, and the kingdom of this world will fully become the kingdom of God. The city of God will be filled with the presence of God and His people. As in the garden of Eden, there will be no need for a temple in this city because "the Lord God the Almighty and the Lamb are its temple" (Rv 21:22).

Sacred to the Lord

EZEKIEL 45

THE SACRED PORTION OF THE LAND

[1] "When you divide the land by lot as an inheritance, set aside a donation to the LORD, a holy portion of the land, 8⅓ miles long and 6⅔ miles wide. This entire region will be holy. [2] In this area there will be a square section for the sanctuary, 875 by 875 feet, with 87½ feet of open space all around it. [3] From this holy portion, you will measure off an area 8⅓ miles long and 3⅓ miles wide, in which the sanctuary, the most holy place, will stand. [4] It will be a holy area of the land to be used by the priests who minister in the sanctuary, who approach to serve the LORD. It will be a place for their houses, as well as a holy area for the sanctuary. [5] There will be another area 8⅓ miles long and 3⅓ miles wide for the Levites who minister in the temple; it will be their possession for towns to live in.

[6] "As the property of the city, set aside an area 1⅔ miles wide and 8⅓ miles long, adjacent to the holy donation of land. It will be for the whole house of Israel. [7] And the prince will have the area on each side of the holy donation of land and the city's property, adjacent to the holy donation and the city's property, stretching to the west on the west side and to the east on the east side. Its length will correspond to one of the tribal portions from the western boundary to the eastern boundary. [8] This will be his land as a possession in Israel. My princes will no longer oppress my people but give the rest of the land to the house of Israel according to their tribes.

[9] "This is what the Lord GOD says: You have gone too far, princes of Israel!

PUT AWAY VIOLENCE AND OPPRESSION AND DO WHAT IS JUST AND RIGHT.

Put an end to your evictions of my people." This is the declaration of the Lord GOD. [10] "You are to have honest scales, an honest dry measure, and an honest liquid measure. [11] The dry measure and the liquid measure will be uniform, with the liquid measure containing 5½ gallons and the dry measure holding half a bushel. Their measurement will be a tenth of the standard larger capacity measure. [12] The shekel will weigh twenty gerahs. Your mina will equal sixty shekels.

THE PEOPLE'S CONTRIBUTION TO THE SACRIFICES

[13] "This is the contribution you are to offer: Three quarts from six bushels of wheat and three quarts from six bushels of barley. [14] The quota of oil in liquid measures will be one percent of every cor. The cor equals ten liquid measures or one standard larger capacity measure, since ten liquid measures equal one standard larger capacity measure. [15] And the quota from the flock is one animal out of every two hundred from the well-watered pastures of Israel. These are for the grain offerings, burnt offerings, and fellowship offerings, to make atonement for the people." This is the declaration of the

Lord God. ¹⁶ "All the people of the land must take part in this contribution for the prince in Israel. ¹⁷ Then the burnt offerings, grain offerings, and drink offerings for the festivals, New Moons, and Sabbaths—for all the appointed times of the house of Israel—will be the prince's responsibility. He will provide the sin offerings, grain offerings, burnt offerings, and fellowship offerings to make atonement on behalf of the house of Israel.

¹⁸ "This is what the Lord God says: In the first month, on the first day of the month, you are to take a young, unblemished bull and purify the sanctuary. ¹⁹ The priest is to take some of the blood from the sin offering and apply it to the temple doorposts, the four corners of the altar's ledge, and the doorposts of the gate of the inner court. ²⁰ You are to do the same thing on the seventh day of the month for everyone who sins unintentionally or through ignorance. In this way you will make atonement for the temple.

²¹ "In the first month, on the fourteenth day of the month, you are to celebrate the Passover, a festival of seven days during which unleavened bread will be eaten. ²² On that day the prince will provide a bull as a sin offering on behalf of himself and all the people of the land. ²³ During the seven days of the festival, he will provide seven bulls and seven rams without blemish as a burnt offering to the Lord on each of the seven days, along with a male goat each day for a sin offering. ²⁴ He will also provide a grain offering of half a bushel per bull and half a bushel per ram, along with a gallon of oil for every half bushel. ²⁵ At the festival that begins on the fifteenth day of the seventh month, he will provide the same things for seven days—the same sin offerings, burnt offerings, grain offerings, and oil."

EZEKIEL 46:1-15

SACRIFICES AT APPOINTED TIMES

¹ "This is what the Lord God says: The gate of the inner court that faces east is to be closed during the six days of work, but it will be opened on the Sabbath day and opened on the day of the New Moon. ² The prince should enter from the outside by way of the gate's portico and stand at the gate's doorpost while the priests sacrifice his burnt offerings and fellowship offerings. He will bow in worship at the gate's threshold and then depart, but the gate is not to be closed until evening. ³ The people of the land will also bow in worship before the Lord at the entrance of that gate on the Sabbaths and New Moons.

⁴ "The burnt offering that the prince presents to the Lord on the Sabbath day is to be six unblemished lambs and an unblemished ram. ⁵ The grain offering will be half a bushel with the ram, and the grain offering with the lambs will be whatever he wants to give, as well as a gallon of oil for every half bushel. ⁶ On the day of the New Moon, the burnt offering is to be a young, unblemished bull, as well as six lambs and a ram without blemish. ⁷ He will provide a grain offering of half a

bushel with the bull, half a bushel with the ram, and whatever he can afford with the lambs, together with a gallon of oil for every half bushel. [8] When the prince enters, he is to go in by way of the gate's portico and go out the same way.

[9] "When the people of the land come before the Lord at the appointed times, whoever enters by way of the north gate to worship is to go out by way of the south gate, and whoever enters by way of the south gate is to go out by way of the north gate. No one may return through the gate by which he entered, but is to go out by the opposite gate. [10] When the people enter, the prince will enter with them, and when they leave, he will leave. [11] At the festivals and appointed times, the grain offering will be half a bushel with the bull, half a bushel with the ram, and whatever he wants to give with the lambs, along with a gallon of oil for every half bushel.

[12] "When the prince makes a freewill offering, whether a burnt offering or a fellowship offering as a freewill offering to the Lord, the gate that faces east is to be opened for him. He is to offer his burnt offering or fellowship offering just as he does on the Sabbath day. Then he will go out, and the gate is to be closed after he leaves.

[13] "You are to offer an unblemished year-old male lamb as a daily burnt offering to the Lord; you will offer it every morning. [14] You are also to prepare a grain offering every morning along with it: three quarts, with one-third of a gallon of oil to moisten the fine flour—a grain offering to the Lord. This is a permanent statute to be observed regularly. [15] They will offer the lamb, the grain offering, and the oil every morning as a regular burnt offering."

♥ GOING DEEPER

MICAH 6:8

Mankind, he has told each of you what is good
and what it is the Lord requires of you:
to act justly,
to love faithfulness,
and to walk humbly with your God.

Notes

There will be life everywhere the river goes.

EZEKIEL 47:9

The Life-Giving River

EZEKIEL 46:16–24

TRANSFER OF ROYAL LANDS

[16] "This is what the Lord GOD says: If the prince gives a gift to each of his sons as their inheritance, it will belong to his sons. It will become their property by inheritance. [17] But if he gives a gift from his inheritance to one of his servants, it will belong to that servant until the year of freedom, when it will revert to the prince. His inheritance belongs only to his sons; it is theirs. [18] The prince must not take any of the people's inheritance, evicting them from their property. He is to provide an inheritance for his sons from his own property, so that none of my people will be displaced from his own property."

THE TEMPLE KITCHENS

[19] Then he brought me through the entrance that was at the side of the gate, into the priests' holy chambers, which faced north. I saw a place there at the far western end. [20] He said to me, "This is the place where the priests will boil the guilt offering and the sin offering, and where they will bake the grain offering, so that they do not bring them into the outer court and transmit holiness to the people." [21] Next he brought me into the outer court and led me past its four corners. There was a separate court in each of its corners. [22] In the four corners of the outer court there were enclosed courts, 70 feet long by 52½ feet wide. All four corner areas had the same dimensions. [23] There was a stone wall around the inside of them, around the four of them, with ovens built at the base of the walls on all sides. [24] He said to me, "These are the kitchens where those who minister at the temple will cook the people's sacrifices."

EZEKIEL 47

THE LIFE-GIVING RIVER

[1] Then he brought me back to the entrance of the temple and there was water flowing from under the threshold of the temple toward the east, for the temple faced east. The water was coming down from under the south side of the threshold of the temple, south of the altar. [2] Next he brought me out by way of the north gate and led me around the outside to the outer gate that faced east; there the water was trickling from the south side. [3] As the man went out east with a measuring line in his hand, he measured off a third of a mile and led me through the water. It came up to my ankles. [4] Then he measured off a third of a mile and led me through the water. It came up to my knees. He measured off another third of a mile and led me through the water. It came up to my waist. [5] Again he measured off a third of a mile, and it was a river that I could not cross on foot. For the water had risen; it was deep enough to swim in, a river that could not be crossed on foot.

[6] He asked me, "Do you see this, son of man?" Then he led me back to the bank of the river. [7] When I had returned, I saw a very large number of trees along both sides of the

riverbank. [8] He said to me, "This water flows out to the eastern region and goes down to the Arabah. When it enters the sea, the sea of foul water, the water of the sea becomes fresh. [9] Every kind of living creature that swarms will live wherever the river flows, and there will be a huge number of fish because this water goes there. Since the water will become fresh, there will be life everywhere the river goes. [10] Fishermen will stand beside it from En-gedi to En-eglaim. These will become places where nets are spread out to dry. Their fish will consist of many different kinds, like the fish of the Mediterranean Sea. [11] Yet its swamps and marshes will not be healed; they will be left for salt. [12] All kinds of trees providing food will grow along both banks of the river. Their leaves will not wither, and their fruit will not fail. Each month they will bear fresh fruit because the water comes from the sanctuary. Their fruit will be used for eating and their leaves for healing."

THE BORDERS OF THE LAND

[13] This is what the Lord GOD says: "This is the border you will use to divide the land as an inheritance for the twelve tribes of Israel. Joseph will receive two shares. [14] You will inherit it in equal portions, since I swore to give it to your ancestors. So this land will fall to you as an inheritance.

[15] This is to be the border of the land:

On the north side it will extend from the Mediterranean Sea by way of Hethlon and Lebo-hamath to Zedad, [16] Berothah, and Sibraim (which is between the border of Damascus and the border of Hamath), as far as Hazer-hatticon, which is on the border of Hauran. [17] So the border will run from the sea to Hazar-enon at the border of Damascus, with the territory of Hamath to the north. This will be the northern side.

[18] On the east side it will run between Hauran and Damascus, along the Jordan between Gilead and the land of Israel; you will measure from the northern border to the eastern sea. This will be the eastern side.

[19] On the south side it will run from Tamar to the Waters of Meribath-kadesh, and on to the Brook of Egypt as far as the Mediterranean Sea. This will be the southern side.

[20] On the west side the Mediterranean Sea will be the border, from the southern border up to a point opposite Lebo-hamath. This will be the western side.

[21] "You are to divide this land among yourselves according to the tribes of Israel. [22] You will allot it as an inheritance for yourselves and for the aliens residing among you, who have fathered children among you. You will treat them like native-born Israelites; along with you, they will be allotted an inheritance among the tribes of Israel. [23] In whatever tribe the alien resides, you will assign his inheritance there." This is the declaration of the Lord GOD.

GOING DEEPER

PSALM 46:4-5

[4] There is a river—
its streams delight the city of God,
the holy dwelling place of the Most High.
[5] God is within her; she will not be toppled.
God will help her when the morning dawns.

JOHN 4:13-14

[13] Jesus said, "Everyone who drinks from this water will get thirsty again. [14] But whoever drinks from the water that I will give him will never get thirsty again. In fact, the water I will give him will become a well of water springing up in him for eternal life."

REVELATION 22:1-2
THE SOURCE OF LIFE

[1] Then he showed me the river of the water of life, clear as crystal, flowing from the throne of God and of the Lamb [2] down the middle of the city's main street. The tree of life was on each side of the river, bearing twelve kinds of fruit, producing its fruit every month. The leaves of the tree are for healing the nations.

Notes

"I will place my Spirit within you
and carefully observe

and cause you to follow my statutes my ordinances." EZEKIEL 36:27

"THE NAME OF THE CITY FROM THAT DAY ON WILL BE THE LORD IS THERE." EZEKIEL 48:35

The New City

EZEKIEL 48

THE TRIBAL ALLOTMENTS

¹ "Now these are the names of the tribes:

From the northern end, along the road of Hethlon, to Lebo-hamath as far as Hazar-enon, at the northern border of Damascus, alongside Hamath and extending from the eastern side to the sea, will be Dan—one portion. ² Next to the territory of Dan, from the east side to the west, will be Asher—one portion. ³ Next to the territory of Asher, from the east side to the west, will be Naphtali—one portion. ⁴ Next to the territory of Naphtali, from the east side to the west, will be Manasseh—one portion. ⁵ Next to the territory of Manasseh, from the east side to the west, will be Ephraim—one portion. ⁶ Next to the territory of Ephraim, from the east side to the west, will be Reuben—one portion. ⁷ Next to the territory of Reuben, from the east side to the west, will be Judah—one portion.

⁸ "Next to the territory of Judah, from the east side to the west, will be the portion you donate to the LORD, 8⅓ miles wide, and as long as one of the tribal portions from the east side to the west. The sanctuary will be in the middle of it.

⁹ "The special portion you donate to the LORD will be 8⅓ miles long and 3⅓ miles wide. ¹⁰ This holy donation will be set apart for the priests alone. It will be 8⅓ miles long on the northern side, 3⅓ miles wide on the western side, 3⅓ miles wide on the eastern side, and 8⅓ miles long on the southern side. The LORD's sanctuary will be in the middle of it. ¹¹ It is for the consecrated priests, the sons of Zadok, who kept my charge and did not go astray as the Levites did when the Israelites went astray. ¹² It will be a special donation for them out of the holy donation of the land, a most holy place adjacent to the territory of the Levites.

¹³ "Next to the territory of the priests, the Levites will have an area 8⅓ miles long and 3⅓ miles wide. The total length will be 8⅓ miles and the width 3⅓ miles. ¹⁴ They must not sell or exchange any of it, and they must not transfer this choice part of the land, for it is holy to the LORD.

¹⁵ "The remaining area, 1⅔ miles wide and 8⅓ miles long, will be for common use by the city, for both residential and open space. The city will be in the middle of it. ¹⁶ These are the city's measurements:

1½ miles on the north side;
1½ miles on the south side;
1½ miles on the east side;
and 1½ miles on the west side.

[17] The city's open space will extend:

425 feet to the north,
425 feet to the south,
425 feet to the east,
and 425 feet to the west.

[18] "The remainder of the length alongside the holy donation will be 3⅓ miles to the east and 3⅓ miles to the west. It will run alongside the holy donation. Its produce will be food for the workers of the city. [19] The city's workers from all the tribes of Israel will cultivate it. [20] The entire donation will be 8⅓ miles by 8⅓ miles; you are to set apart the holy donation along with the city property as a square area.

[21] "The remaining area on both sides of the holy donation and the city property will belong to the prince. He will own the land adjacent to the tribal portions, next to the 8⅓ miles of the donation as far as the eastern border and next to the 8⅓ miles of the donation as far as the western border. The holy donation and the sanctuary of the temple will be in the middle of it. [22] Except for the Levitical property and the city property in the middle of the area belonging to the prince, the area between the territory of Judah and that of Benjamin will belong to the prince.

[23] "As for the rest of the tribes:

From the east side to the west, will be Benjamin—one portion.
[24] Next to the territory of Benjamin, from the east side to the west, will be Simeon—one portion.
[25] Next to the territory of Simeon, from the east side to the west, will be Issachar—one portion.
[26] Next to the territory of Issachar, from the east side to the west, will be Zebulun—one portion.
[27] Next to the territory of Zebulun, from the east side to the west, will be Gad—one portion.

[28] Next to the territory of Gad toward the south side, the border will run from Tamar to the Waters of Meribath-kadesh, to the Brook of Egypt, and out to the Mediterranean Sea. [29] This is the land you are to allot as an inheritance to Israel's tribes, and these will be their portions." This is the declaration of the Lord God.

30 "These are the exits of the city:

> On the north side, which measures 1½ miles, 31 there will be three gates facing north, the gates of the city being named for the tribes of Israel: one, the gate of Reuben; one, the gate of Judah; and one, the gate of Levi.
>
> 32 On the east side, which is 1½ miles, there will be three gates: one, the gate of Joseph; one, the gate of Benjamin; and one, the gate of Dan.
>
> 33 On the south side, which measures 1½ miles, there will be three gates: one, the gate of Simeon; one, the gate of Issachar; and one, the gate of Zebulun.
>
> 34 On the west side, which is 1½ miles, there will be three gates: one, the gate of Gad; one, the gate of Asher; and one, the gate of Naphtali.

35 The perimeter of the city will be six miles, and the name of the city from that day on will be The LORD Is There."

🔖 GOING DEEPER

ZECHARIAH 2:10

"Daughter Zion, shout for joy and be glad, for I am coming to dwell among you"—this is the LORD's declaration.

REVELATION 21:3, 10-22

3 Then I heard a loud voice from the throne: Look, God's dwelling is with humanity, and he will live with them. They will be his peoples, and God himself will be with them and will be their God.

...

10 He then carried me away in the Spirit to a great, high mountain and showed me the holy city, Jerusalem, coming down out of heaven from God, 11 arrayed with God's glory. Her radiance was like a precious jewel, like a jasper stone, clear as crystal. 12 The city had a massive high wall, with twelve gates. Twelve angels were at the gates; the names of the twelve tribes of Israel's sons were inscribed on the gates. 13 There were three gates on the east, three gates on the north, three gates on the south, and three gates on the west. 14 The city wall had twelve foundations, and the twelve names of the twelve apostles of the Lamb were on the foundations.

15 The one who spoke with me had a golden measuring rod to measure the city, its gates, and its wall. 16 The city is laid out in a square; its length and width are the same. He measured the city with the rod at 12,000 *stadia*. Its length, width, and height are equal. 17 Then he measured its wall, 144 cubits according to human measurement, which the angel used. 18 The building material of its wall was jasper, and the city was pure gold clear as glass. 19 The foundations of the city wall were adorned with every kind of jewel: the first foundation is jasper, the second sapphire, the third chalcedony, the fourth emerald, 20 the fifth sardonyx, the sixth carnelian, the seventh chrysolite, the eighth beryl, the ninth topaz, the tenth chrysoprase, the eleventh jacinth, the twelfth amethyst. 21 The twelve gates are twelve pearls; each individual gate was made of a single pearl. The main street of the city was pure gold, transparent as glass.

22 I DID NOT SEE A TEMPLE IN IT, BECAUSE THE LORD GOD THE ALMIGHTY AND THE LAMB ARE ITS TEMPLE.

Response

LAMENT

During this Lenten season, we make time to lament— to grieve our own sin and express sorrow over the brokenness of the world, to which our sin contributes.

1 What in your life do you need to lament? Take time to confess your own sin and grieve over how the sin of others has affected you.

2 How does your sin and brokenness affect your community? Take time to lament for the brokenness you see in the world.

CONFESSION
AND ASSURANCE

A lament is not a quick
fix, but God is faithful,
and lamenting gently but
persistently reminds us to
trust Him. Use this space to
confess your need for God
and His intervention, as well
as express your continued
hope found in His provision.

Blood Orange and Honey-glazed Ham

SERVES 12

INGREDIENTS

1 (8- to 10-pound) bone-in, skin-on smoked uncured ham

Fine sea salt and freshly ground black pepper

½ cup ghee, grass-fed unsalted butter, or coconut oil

Finely grated zest and juice of 3 blood oranges

½ cup light-colored raw honey

¼ cup whole-grain mustard

8 fresh sage leaves

¼ teaspoon ground cloves

¼ teaspoon ground cinnamon

2 pounds baby carrots, cleaned and trimmed

1 blood orange, sliced, for garnish (optional)

DIRECTIONS

Preheat the oven to 300°F.

Using a sharp knife, score the skin and fat of the ham in a 2-inch diamond pattern. Place the ham fat side up on a roasting rack in a roasting pan. Season the meat generously with salt and pepper. Bake the ham for 1½ hours.

Meanwhile, make the glaze. Combine the ghee, orange juice, orange zest, honey, mustard, sage, cloves, and cinnamon in a small saucepan. Simmer for 30 minutes, or until the mixture has thickened into a syrup.

Increase the oven temperature to 350°F and remove the roasting pan. Season the carrots with salt and pepper and scatter them around the bottom of the roasting pan. Baste the ham with the glaze and return the pan to the oven. Bake for another 30 minutes, basting occasionally, until a meat thermometer inserted into the center of the ham reads 135°F and the carrots are tender.

Transfer the ham to a cutting board, cover, and let it rest for 20 minutes before carving. Serve the carrots on the side and place slices of blood orange decoratively around the platter for garnish.

MAKE IT AHEAD

Make the glaze 3 days in advance and store it in an airtight container in the refrigerator. Reheat the glaze in a saucepan over low heat. Season the ham and place it in the roasting pan, covered with plastic wrap, in the refrigerator the night before. Clean and trim the carrots up to 2 days in advance and store them in a bowl of water, tightly covered, in the refrigerator. Alternatively, bake and slice the ham the morning of the brunch and spoon the juices onto the bottom of a platter. Arrange the ham and carrots on top, then cover and leave at room temperature for up to 2 hours. Reheat in a low oven just prior to serving.

Rebecca Hunter, *Winter Sowing*, 2021, oil on canvas, 24x36 in.

GRACE DAY

"I will have compassion on you with everlasting love," says the LORD your Redeemer.

ISAIAH 54:8

DAY 41

Lent is a season where we reflect on the depth of our sin and embrace the hope and strength found only in the cross of Christ. We seek unhurried moments of quiet to read Scripture, pray, confess, and repent. Take some time today to catch up on your reading, make space for prayer, and rest in God's presence.

INTRODUCTION
TO HOLY WEEK

Over the last six weeks as we read the book of Ezekiel, we reflected on the nature of sin and confessed our need for a Savior, someone who would replace our hearts of stone with hearts of flesh. Now we pivot our attention to the climax of this redemption story: when Jesus, our promised, desperately needed Savior, sacrificed Himself on the cross for our sins and rose from the dead.

This last week of our Lenten reading plan walks through the final week of Jesus's life on earth—from His triumphant entry into the city of Jerusalem to His death on the cross, His days in the tomb, and His magnificent resurrection on Easter Sunday.

Spend this week remembering the weight of sin and judgment Jesus came to bear, and rejoicing in the gift of new life He offers to our dry, weary bones.

Palm Sunday

LUKE 19:28–44

THE TRIUMPHAL ENTRY

28 When he had said these things, he went on ahead, going up to Jerusalem. 29 As he approached Bethphage and Bethany, at the place called the Mount of Olives, he sent two of the disciples 30 and said, "Go into the village ahead of you. As you enter it, you will find a colt tied there, on which no one has ever sat. Untie it and bring it. 31 If anyone asks you, 'Why are you untying it?' say this: 'The Lord needs it.'"

32 So those who were sent left and found it just as he had told them. 33 As they were untying the colt, its owners said to them, "Why are you untying the colt?"

34 "The Lord needs it," they said. 35 Then they brought it to Jesus, and after throwing their clothes on the colt, they helped Jesus get on it. 36 As he was going along, they were spreading their clothes on the road. 37 Now he came near the path down the Mount of Olives, and the whole crowd of the disciples began to praise God joyfully with a loud voice for all the miracles they had seen:

38 Blessed is the King who comes
in the name of the Lord.
Peace in heaven
and glory in the highest heaven!

39 Some of the Pharisees from the crowd told him, "Teacher, rebuke your disciples."

40 He answered, "I tell you, if they were to keep silent, the stones would cry out."

JESUS'S LOVE FOR JERUSALEM

41 As he approached and saw the city, he wept for it, 42 saying, "If you knew this day what would bring peace—but now it is hidden from your eyes. 43 For the days will come on you when your enemies will build a barricade around you, surround you, and hem you in on every side. 44 They will crush you and your children among you to the ground, and they will not leave one stone on another in your midst, because you did not recognize the time when God visited you."

GOING DEEPER

PSALM 118:25–29

25 Lord, save us!
Lord, please grant us success!
26 He who comes in the name
of the Lord is blessed.

From the house of the LORD we bless you.
²⁷ The LORD is God and has given us light.
Bind the festival sacrifice with cords
to the horns of the altar.
²⁸ You are my God, and I will give you thanks.
You are my God; I will exalt you.
²⁹ Give thanks to the LORD, for he is good;
his faithful love endures forever.

ZECHARIAH 9:9

Rejoice greatly, Daughter Zion!
Shout in triumph, Daughter Jerusalem!

LOOK, YOUR KING IS COMING TO YOU;
HE IS RIGHTEOUS AND VICTORIOUS,

humble and riding on a donkey,
on a colt, the foal of a donkey.

Notes

DAY 42

Cleansing the Temple

MARK 11:12-19

THE BARREN FIG TREE IS CURSED

¹² The next day when they went out from Bethany, he was hungry. ¹³ Seeing in the distance a fig tree with leaves, he went to find out if there was anything on it. When he came to it, he found nothing but leaves; for it was not the season for figs. ¹⁴ He said to it, "May no one ever eat fruit from you again!" And his disciples heard it.

CLEANSING THE TEMPLE

¹⁵ They came to Jerusalem, and he went into the temple and began to throw out those buying and selling. He overturned the tables of the money changers and the chairs of those selling doves, ¹⁶ and would not permit anyone to carry goods through the temple. ¹⁷ He was teaching them: "Is it not written, My house will be called a house of prayer for all nations? But you have made it a den of thieves!"

¹⁸ The chief priests and the scribes heard it and started looking for a way to kill him. For they were afraid of him, because the whole crowd was astonished by his teaching.

¹⁹ Whenever evening came, they would go out of the city.

◖ GOING DEEPER

ISAIAH 56:1-8

A HOUSE OF PRAYER FOR ALL

¹ This is what the LORD says:

Preserve justice and do what is right,
for my salvation is coming soon,
and my righteousness will be revealed.
² Happy is the person who does this,
the son of man who holds it fast,
who keeps the Sabbath without desecrating it,
and keeps his hand from doing any evil.

³ No foreigner who has joined himself to the LORD
should say,
"The LORD will exclude me from his people,"
and the eunuch should not say,
"Look, I am a dried-up tree."
⁴ For the LORD says this:
"For the eunuchs who keep my Sabbaths,
and choose what pleases me,
and hold firmly to my covenant,
⁵ I will give them, in my house and within my walls,
a memorial and a name
better than sons and daughters.
I will give each of them an everlasting name
that will never be cut off.
⁶ As for the foreigners who join themselves to the LORD
to minister to him, to love the name of the LORD,
and to become his servants—
all who keep the Sabbath without desecrating it
and who hold firmly to my covenant—
⁷ I will bring them to my holy mountain
and let them rejoice in my house of prayer.
Their burnt offerings and sacrifices
will be acceptable on my altar,
for my house will be called a house of prayer
for all nations."
⁸ This is the declaration of the Lord GOD,
who gathers the dispersed of Israel:
"I will gather to them still others
besides those already gathered."

"They will see the Son of Man coming in a cloud with power and great glory."

LUKE 21:27

The Coming of the Son of Man

LUKE 21

THE WIDOW'S GIFT

[1] He looked up and saw the rich dropping their offerings into the temple treasury. [2] He also saw a poor widow dropping in two tiny coins. [3] "Truly I tell you," he said, "this poor widow has put in more than all of them. [4] For all these people have put in gifts out of their surplus, but she out of her poverty has put in all she had to live on."

DESTRUCTION OF THE TEMPLE PREDICTED

[5] As some were talking about the temple, how it was adorned with beautiful stones and gifts dedicated to God, he said, [6] "These things that you see—the days will come when not one stone will be left on another that will not be thrown down."

SIGNS OF THE END OF THE AGE

[7] "Teacher," they asked him, "so when will these things happen? And what will be the sign when these things are about to take place?"

[8] Then he said, "Watch out that you are not deceived. For many will come in my name, saying, 'I am he,' and, 'The time is near.' Don't follow them. [9] When you hear of wars and rebellions, don't be alarmed. Indeed, it is necessary that these things take place first, but the end won't come right away."

[10] Then he told them, "Nation will be raised up against nation, and kingdom against kingdom. [11] There will be violent earthquakes, and famines and plagues in various places, and there will be terrifying sights and great signs from heaven. [12] But before all these things, they will lay their hands on you and persecute you. They will hand you over to the synagogues and prisons, and you will be brought before kings and governors because of my name. [13] This will give you an opportunity to bear witness. [14] Therefore make up your minds not to prepare your defense ahead of time, [15] for I will give you such words and a wisdom that none of your adversaries will be able to resist or contradict. [16] You will even be betrayed by parents, brothers, relatives, and friends. They will kill some of you. [17] You will be hated by everyone because of my name, [18] but not a hair of your head will be lost. [19] By your endurance, gain your lives.

THE DESTRUCTION OF JERUSALEM

[20] "When you see Jerusalem surrounded by armies, then recognize that its desolation has come near. [21] Then those in Judea must flee to the mountains. Those inside the city must leave it, and those who are in the country must not enter it, [22] because these are days of vengeance to fulfill all

the things that are written. ²³ Woe to pregnant women and nursing mothers in those days, for there will be great distress in the land and wrath against this people. ²⁴ They will be killed by the sword and be led captive into all the nations, and Jerusalem will be trampled by the Gentiles until the times of the Gentiles are fulfilled.

THE COMING OF THE SON OF MAN

²⁵ "Then there will be signs in the sun, moon, and stars; and there will be anguish on the earth among nations bewildered by the roaring of the sea and the waves. ²⁶ People will faint from fear and expectation of the things that are coming on the world, because the powers of the heavens will be shaken.

²⁷ THEN THEY WILL SEE THE SON OF MAN COMING IN A CLOUD WITH POWER AND GREAT GLORY. ²⁸ BUT WHEN THESE THINGS BEGIN TO TAKE PLACE, STAND UP AND LIFT YOUR HEADS, BECAUSE YOUR REDEMPTION IS NEAR."

THE PARABLE OF THE FIG TREE

²⁹ Then he told them a parable: "Look at the fig tree, and all the trees. ³⁰ As soon as they put out leaves you can see for yourselves and recognize that summer is already near. ³¹ In the same way, when you see these things happening, recognize that the kingdom of God is near. ³² Truly I tell you, this generation will certainly not pass away until all things take place. ³³ Heaven and earth will pass away, but my words will never pass away.

THE NEED FOR WATCHFULNESS

³⁴ "Be on your guard, so that your minds are not dulled from carousing, drunkenness, and worries of life, or that day will come on you unexpectedly ³⁵ like a trap. For it will come on all who live on the face of the whole earth. ³⁶ But be alert at all times, praying that you may have strength to escape all these things that are going to take place and to stand before the Son of Man."

³⁷ During the day, he was teaching in the temple, but in the evening he would go out and spend the night on what is called the Mount of Olives. ³⁸ Then all the people would come early in the morning to hear him in the temple.

LUKE 22:1-2

THE PLOT TO KILL JESUS

¹ The Festival of Unleavened Bread, which is called Passover, was approaching. ² The chief priests and the scribes were looking for a way to put him to death, because they were afraid of the people.

🔖 GOING DEEPER

DANIEL 7:13-14

¹³ I continued watching in the night visions,

and suddenly one like a son of man
was coming with the clouds of heaven.
He approached the Ancient of Days
and was escorted before him.
¹⁴ He was given dominion
and glory and a kingdom,
so that those of every people,
nation, and language
should serve him.
His dominion is an everlasting dominion
that will not pass away,
and his kingdom is one
that will not be destroyed.

Notes

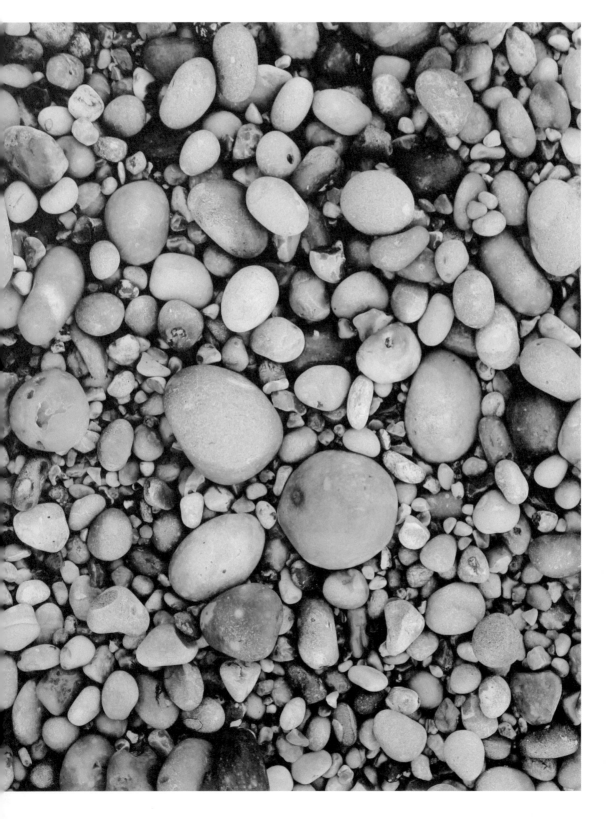

"WHEREVER THE GOSPEL IS PROCLAIMED IN THE WHOLE WORLD, WHAT SHE HAS DONE WILL ALSO BE TOLD IN MEMORY OF HER." MARK 14:9

The Anointing at Bethany

MATTHEW 26:14-16

¹⁴ Then one of the Twelve, the man called Judas Iscariot, went to the chief priests ¹⁵ and said, "What are you willing to give me if I hand him over to you?" So they weighed out thirty pieces of silver for him. ¹⁶ And from that time he started looking for a good opportunity to betray him.

MARK 14:3-11

THE ANOINTING AT BETHANY

³ While he was in Bethany at the house of Simon the leper, as he was reclining at the table, a woman came with an alabaster jar of very expensive perfume of pure nard. She broke the jar and poured it on his head. ⁴ But some were expressing indignation to one another: "Why has this perfume been wasted? ⁵ For this perfume might have been sold for more than three hundred denarii and given to the poor." And they began to scold her.

⁶ Jesus replied, "Leave her alone. Why are you bothering her? She has done a noble thing for me. ⁷ You always have the poor with you, and you can do what is good for them whenever you want, but you do not always have me. ⁸ She has done what she could; she has anointed my body in advance for burial. ⁹ Truly I tell you, wherever the gospel is proclaimed in the whole world, what she has done will also be told in memory of her."

¹⁰ Then Judas Iscariot, one of the Twelve, went to the chief priests to betray Jesus to them. ¹¹ And when they heard this, they were glad and promised to give him money. So he started looking for a good opportunity to betray him.

🔖 GOING DEEPER

LUKE 22:3-6

³ Then Satan entered Judas, called Iscariot, who was numbered among the Twelve. ⁴ He went away and discussed with the chief priests and temple police how he could hand him over to them. ⁵ They were glad and agreed to give him silver. ⁶ So he accepted the offer and started looking for a good opportunity to betray him to them when the crowd was not present.

SHE READS TRUTH   DAY 45   215

The Lost Supper

46

PREPARATION FOR PASSOVER

12 On the first day of Unleavened Bread, when they sacrifice the Passover lamb, his disciples asked him, "Where do you want us to go and prepare the Passover so that you may eat it?"

13 So he sent two of his disciples and told them, "Go into the city, and a man carrying a jar of water will meet you. Follow him. 14 Wherever he enters, tell the owner of the house, 'The Teacher says, "Where is my guest room where I may eat the Passover with my disciples?"' 15 He will show you a large room upstairs, furnished and ready. Make the preparations for us there." 16 So the disciples went out, entered the city, and found it just as he had told them, and they prepared the Passover.

BETRAYAL AT THE PASSOVER

17 When evening came, he arrived with the Twelve. 18 While they were reclining and eating, Jesus said, "Truly I tell you, one of you will betray me—one who is eating with me."

19 They began to be distressed and to say to him one by one, "Surely not I?"

20 He said to them, "It is one of the Twelve—the one who is dipping bread in the bowl with me. 21 For the Son of Man will go just as it is written about him, but woe to that man by whom the Son of Man is betrayed! It would have been better for him if he had not been born."

THE FIRST LORD'S SUPPER

22 AS THEY WERE EATING, HE TOOK BREAD, BLESSED AND BROKE IT, GAVE IT TO THEM, AND SAID, "TAKE IT; THIS IS MY BODY."

23 Then he took a cup, and after giving thanks, he gave it to them, and they all drank from it. 24 He said to them, "This is my blood of the covenant, which is poured out for many. 25 Truly I tell you, I will no longer drink of the fruit of the vine until that day when I drink it new in the kingdom of God."

26 After singing a hymn, they went out to the Mount of Olives.

PETER'S DENIAL PREDICTED

27 Then Jesus said to them, "All of you will fall away, because it is written:

> I will strike the shepherd,
> and the sheep will be scattered.

28 But after I have risen, I will go ahead of you to Galilee."

29 Peter told him, "Even if everyone falls away, I will not."

30 "Truly I tell you," Jesus said to him, "today, this very night, before the rooster crows twice, you will deny me three times."

31 But he kept insisting, "If I have to die with you, I will never deny you." And they all said the same thing.

THE PRAYER IN THE GARDEN

32 Then they came to a place named Gethsemane, and he told his disciples, "Sit here while I pray." 33 He took Peter, James, and John with him, and he began to be deeply distressed and troubled. 34 He said to them, "I am deeply grieved to the point of death. Remain here and stay awake." 35 He went a little farther, fell to the ground, and prayed that if it were possible, the hour might pass from him. 36 And he said, "*Abba*, Father! All things are possible for you. Take this cup away from me. Nevertheless, not what I will, but what you will." 37 Then he came and found them sleeping. He said to Peter, "Simon, are you sleeping? Couldn't you stay awake one hour? 38 Stay awake and pray so that you won't enter into temptation. The spirit is willing, but the flesh is weak." 39 Once again he went away and prayed, saying the same thing. 40 And again he came and found them sleeping, because they could not keep their eyes open. They did not know what to say to him. 41 Then he came a third time and said to them, "Are you still sleeping and resting? Enough! The time has come. See, the Son of Man is betrayed into the hands of sinners. 42 Get up; let's go. See, my betrayer is near."

JUDAS'S BETRAYAL OF JESUS

43 While he was still speaking, Judas, one of the Twelve, suddenly arrived. With him was a mob, with swords and

clubs, from the chief priests, the scribes, and the elders. [44] His betrayer had given them a signal. "The one I kiss," he said, "he's the one; arrest him and take him away under guard." [45] So when he came, immediately he went up to Jesus and said, "Rabbi!" and kissed him. [46] They took hold of him and arrested him. [47] One of those who stood by drew his sword, struck the high priest's servant, and cut off his ear.

[48] Jesus said to them, "Have you come out with swords and clubs, as if I were a criminal, to capture me? [49] Every day I was among you, teaching in the temple, and you didn't arrest me. But the Scriptures must be fulfilled."

[50] Then they all deserted him and ran away. [51] Now a certain young man, wearing nothing but a linen cloth, was following him. They caught hold of him, [52] but he left the linen cloth behind and ran away naked.

JESUS FACES THE SANHEDRIN

[53] They led Jesus away to the high priest, and all the chief priests, the elders, and the scribes assembled. [54] Peter followed him at a distance, right into the high priest's courtyard. He was sitting with the servants, warming himself by the fire.

[55] The chief priests and the whole Sanhedrin were looking for testimony against Jesus to put him to death, but they could not find any. [56] For many were giving false testimony against him, and the testimonies did not agree. [57] Some stood up and gave false testimony against him, stating, [58] "We heard him say, 'I will destroy this temple made with human hands, and in three days I will build another not made by hands.'" [59] Yet their testimony did not agree even on this.

[60] Then the high priest stood up before them all and questioned Jesus, "Don't you have an answer to what these men are testifying against you?" [61] But he kept silent and did not answer. Again the high priest questioned him, "Are you the Messiah, the Son of the Blessed One?"

[62] "I am," said Jesus, "and you will see the Son of Man seated at the right hand of Power and coming with the clouds of heaven."

[63] Then the high priest tore his robes and said, "Why do we still need witnesses? [64] You have heard the blasphemy. What is your decision?" They all condemned him as deserving death.

[65] Then some began to spit on him, to blindfold him, and to beat him, saying, "Prophesy!" The temple servants also took him and slapped him.

PETER DENIES HIS LORD

[66] While Peter was in the courtyard below, one of the high priest's maidservants came. [67] When she saw Peter warming himself, she looked at him and said, "You also were with Jesus, the man from Nazareth."

[68] But he denied it: "I don't know or understand what you're talking about." Then he went out to the entryway, and a rooster crowed.

[69] When the maidservant saw him again, she began to tell those standing nearby, "This man is one of them."

[70] But again he denied it. After a little while those standing there said to Peter again, "You certainly are one of them, since you're also a Galilean."

[71] Then he started to curse and swear, "I don't know this man you're talking about!"

[72] Immediately a rooster crowed a second time, and Peter remembered when Jesus had spoken the word to him, "Before the rooster crows twice, you will deny me three times." And he broke down and wept.

JOHN 16:16–24

SORROW TURNED TO JOY

[16] "In a little while, you will no longer see me; again in a little while, you will see me."

[17] Then some of his disciples said to one another, "What is this he's telling us: 'In a little while, you will not see me; again in a little while, you will see me,' and, 'Because I am going

to the Father'?" [18] They said, "What is this he is saying, 'In a little while'? We don't know what he's talking about."

[19] Jesus knew they wanted to ask him, and so he said to them, "Are you asking one another about what I said, 'In a little while, you will not see me; again in a little while, you will see me'? [20] Truly I tell you, you will weep and mourn, but the world will rejoice. You will become sorrowful, but your sorrow will turn to joy. [21] When a woman is in labor, she has pain because her time has come. But when she has given birth to a child, she no longer remembers the suffering because of the joy that a person has been born into the world. [22] So you also have sorrow now. But I will see you again. Your hearts will rejoice, and no one will take away your joy from you.

[23] "In that day you will not ask me anything. Truly I tell you, anything you ask the Father in my name, he will give you. [24] Until now you have asked for nothing in my name. Ask and you will receive, so that your joy may be complete."

◆ GOING DEEPER

PSALM 41:7–13

[7] All who hate me whisper together about me;
they plan to harm me.
[8] "Something awful has overwhelmed him,
and he won't rise again from where he lies!"
[9] Even my friend in whom I trusted,
one who ate my bread,
has raised his heel against me.

[10] But you, Lord, be gracious to me and raise me up;
then I will repay them.
[11] By this I know that you delight in me:
my enemy does not shout in triumph over me.
[12] You supported me because of my integrity
and set me in your presence forever.

[13] Blessed be the Lord God of Israel,
from everlasting to everlasting.
Amen and amen.

Good Friday

MARK 15

JESUS FACES PILATE

[1] As soon as it was morning, having held a meeting with the elders, scribes, and the whole Sanhedrin, the chief priests tied Jesus up, led him away, and handed him over to Pilate.

[2] So Pilate asked him, "Are you the king of the Jews?"

He answered him, "You say so."

[3] And the chief priests accused him of many things. [4] Pilate questioned him again, "Aren't you going to answer? Look how many things they are accusing you of!" [5] But Jesus still did not answer, and so Pilate was amazed.

JESUS OR BARABBAS

[6] At the festival Pilate used to release for the people a prisoner whom they requested. [7] There was one named Barabbas, who was in prison with rebels who had committed murder during the rebellion. [8] The crowd came up and began to ask Pilate to do for them as was his custom. [9] Pilate answered them, "Do you want me to release the king of the Jews for you?" [10] For he knew it was because of envy that the chief priests had handed him over. [11] But the chief priests stirred up the crowd so that he would release Barabbas to them instead. [12] Pilate asked them again, "Then what do you want me to do with the one you call the king of the Jews?"

[13] Again they shouted, "Crucify him!"

[14] Pilate said to them, "Why? What has he done wrong?"

But they shouted all the more, "Crucify him!"

[15] Wanting to satisfy the crowd, Pilate released Barabbas to them; and after having Jesus flogged, he handed him over to be crucified.

MOCKED BY THE MILITARY

[16] The soldiers led him away into the palace (that is, the governor's residence) and called the whole company together. [17] They dressed him in a purple robe, twisted together a crown of thorns, and put it on him. [18] And they began to salute him, "Hail, king of the Jews!" [19] They were hitting him on the head with a stick and spitting on him. Getting down on their knees, they were paying him homage. [20] After they

had mocked him, they stripped him of the purple robe and put his clothes on him.

CRUCIFIED BETWEEN TWO CRIMINALS

They led him out to crucify him. [21] They forced a man coming in from the country, who was passing by, to carry Jesus's cross. He was Simon of Cyrene, the father of Alexander and Rufus.

[22] They brought Jesus to the place called *Golgotha* (which means Place of the Skull). [23] They tried to give him wine mixed with myrrh, but he did not take it.

[24] Then they crucified him and divided his clothes, casting lots for them to decide what each would get. [25] Now it was nine in the morning when they crucified him. [26] The inscription of the charge written against him was: THE KING OF THE JEWS. [27] They crucified two criminals with him, one on his right and one on his left.

[29] Those who passed by were yelling insults at him, shaking their heads, and saying, "Ha! The one who would destroy the temple and rebuild it in three days, [30] save yourself by coming down from the cross!" [31] In the same way, the chief priests with the scribes were mocking him among themselves and saying, "He saved others, but he cannot save himself! [32] Let the Messiah, the King of Israel, come down now from the cross, so that we may see and believe." Even those who were crucified with him taunted him.

THE DEATH OF JESUS

[33] When it was noon, darkness came over the whole land until three in the afternoon. [34] And at three Jesus cried out with a loud voice, *"Eloi, Eloi, lemá sabachtháni?"* which is translated, "My God, my God, why have you abandoned me?"

[35] When some of those standing there heard this, they said, "See, he's calling for Elijah."

[36] Someone ran and filled a sponge with sour wine, fixed it on a stick, offered him a drink, and said, "Let's see if Elijah comes to take him down."

[37] Jesus let out a loud cry and breathed his last. [38] Then the curtain of the temple was torn in two from top to bottom. [39] When the centurion, who was standing opposite him, saw the way he breathed his last, he said,

"TRULY THIS MAN WAS THE SON OF GOD!"

[40] There were also women watching from a distance. Among them were Mary Magdalene, Mary the mother of James the younger and of Joses, and Salome. [41] In Galilee these women followed him and took care of him. Many other women had come up with him to Jerusalem.

THE BURIAL OF JESUS

[42] When it was already evening, because it was the day of preparation (that is, the day before the Sabbath), [43] Joseph of Arimathea, a prominent member of the Sanhedrin who was himself looking forward to the kingdom of God, came and boldly went to Pilate and asked for Jesus's body. [44] Pilate was surprised that he was already dead. Summoning the centurion, he asked him whether he had already died. [45] When he found out from the centurion, he gave the corpse to Joseph. [46] After he bought some linen cloth, Joseph took him down and wrapped him in the linen. Then he laid him in a tomb cut out of the rock and rolled a stone against the entrance to the tomb. [47] Mary Magdalene and Mary the mother of Joses were watching where he was laid.

◖ GOING DEEPER

ISAIAH 52:13–15

THE SERVANT'S SUFFERING AND EXALTATION

[13] See, my servant will be successful;
he will be raised and lifted up and greatly exalted.
[14] Just as many were appalled at you—
his appearance was so disfigured
that he did not look like a man,
and his form did not resemble a human being—
[15] so he will sprinkle many nations.
Kings will shut their mouths because of him,
for they will see what had not been told them,
and they will understand what they had not heard.

ISAIAH 53:1-7

¹ Who has believed what we have heard?
And to whom has the arm of the LORD been revealed?
² He grew up before him like a young plant
and like a root out of dry ground.
He didn't have an impressive form
or majesty that we should look at him,
no appearance that we should desire him.
³ He was despised and rejected by men,
a man of suffering who knew what sickness was.
He was like someone people turned away from;
he was despised, and we didn't value him.

⁴ Yet he himself bore our sicknesses,
and he carried our pains;
but we in turn regarded him stricken,
struck down by God, and afflicted.
⁵ But he was pierced because of our rebellion,
crushed because of our iniquities;
punishment for our peace was on him,
and we are healed by his wounds.
⁶ We all went astray like sheep;
we all have turned to our own way;
and the LORD has punished him
for the iniquity of us all.

⁷ He was oppressed and afflicted,
yet he did not open his mouth.
Like a lamb led to the slaughter
and like a sheep silent before her shearers,
he did not open his mouth.

Notes

Just As I Am

WORDS
Charlotte Elliott

MUSIC
William B. Bradbury

Holy Saturday

MATTHEW 27:62-66

THE CLOSELY GUARDED TOMB

⁶² The next day, which followed the preparation day, the chief priests and the Pharisees gathered before Pilate ⁶³ and said, "Sir, we remember that while this deceiver was still alive he said, 'After three days I will rise again.'

⁶⁴ SO GIVE ORDERS THAT THE TOMB BE MADE SECURE UNTIL THE THIRD DAY.

Otherwise, his disciples may come, steal him, and tell the people, 'He has been raised from the dead,' and the last deception will be worse than the first."

⁶⁵ "Take guards," Pilate told them. "Go and make it as secure as you know how." ⁶⁶ They went and secured the tomb by setting a seal on the stone and placing the guards.

LUKE 23:54-56

⁵⁴ It was the preparation day, and the Sabbath was about to begin. ⁵⁵ The women who had come with him from Galilee followed along and observed the tomb and how his body was placed. ⁵⁶ Then they returned and prepared spices and perfumes. And they rested on the Sabbath according to the commandment.

GOING DEEPER

ISAIAH 53:8-12

⁸ He was taken away because of oppression and judgment;
and who considered his fate?
For he was cut off from the land of the living;
he was struck because of my people's rebellion.
⁹ He was assigned a grave with the wicked,
but he was with a rich man at his death,
because he had done no violence
and had not spoken deceitfully.

¹⁰ Yet the LORD was pleased to crush him severely.
When you make him a guilt offering,
he will see his seed, he will prolong his days,
and by his hand, the LORD's pleasure will be accomplished.
¹¹ After his anguish,
he will see light and be satisfied.
By his knowledge,
my righteous servant will justify many,
and he will carry their iniquities.
¹² Therefore I will give him the many as a portion,
and he will receive the mighty as spoil,
because he willingly submitted to death,
and was counted among the rebels;
yet he bore the sin of many
and interceded for the rebels.

He is not here,
but he has risen!

LUKE 24:6

Easter Sunday

LUKE 24:1-49

RESURRECTION MORNING

¹ On the first day of the week, very early in the morning, they came to the tomb, bringing the spices they had prepared. ² They found the stone rolled away from the tomb. ³ They went in but did not find the body of the Lord Jesus. ⁴ While they were perplexed about this, suddenly two men stood by them in dazzling clothes. ⁵ So the women were terrified and bowed down to the ground.

"Why are you looking for the living among the dead?" asked the men. ⁶ "He is not here, but he has risen! Remember how he spoke to you when he was still in Galilee, ⁷ saying, 'It is necessary that the Son of Man be betrayed into the hands of sinful men, be crucified, and rise on the third day'?" ⁸ And they remembered his words.

⁹ Returning from the tomb, they reported all these things to the Eleven and to all the rest. ¹⁰ Mary Magdalene, Joanna, Mary the mother of James, and the other women with them were telling the apostles these things. ¹¹ But these words seemed like nonsense to them, and they did not believe the women. ¹² Peter, however, got up and ran to the tomb. When he stooped to look in, he saw only the linen cloths. So he went away, amazed at what had happened.

THE EMMAUS DISCIPLES

¹³ Now that same day two of them were on their way to a village called Emmaus, which was about seven miles from Jerusalem. ¹⁴ Together they were discussing everything that had taken place. ¹⁵ And while they were discussing and arguing, Jesus himself came near and began to walk along with them. ¹⁶ But they were prevented from recognizing him. ¹⁷ Then he asked them, "What is this dispute that you're having with each other as you are walking?" And they stopped walking and looked discouraged.

¹⁸ The one named Cleopas answered him, "Are you the only visitor in Jerusalem who doesn't know the things that happened there in these days?"

¹⁹ "What things?" he asked them.

So they said to him, "The things concerning Jesus of Nazareth, who was a prophet powerful in action and speech before God and all the people, ²⁰ and how our chief priests and leaders handed him over to be sentenced to death, and they crucified him. ²¹ But we were hoping that he was the one who was about to redeem Israel. Besides all this, it's the third day since these things happened. ²² Moreover, some women from our group astounded us. They arrived early at the tomb, 23 and when they didn't find his body, they came and reported that they had seen a vision of angels who said he was alive. 24 Some of those who were with us went to the tomb and found it just as the women had said, but they didn't see him."

25 He said to them, "How foolish you are, and how slow to believe all that the prophets have spoken! 26 Wasn't it necessary for the Messiah to suffer these things and enter into his glory?" 27 Then beginning with Moses and all the Prophets, he interpreted for them the things concerning himself in all the Scriptures.

28 They came near the village where they were going, and he gave the impression that he was going farther. 29 But they urged him, "Stay with us, because it's almost evening, and now the day is almost over." So he went in to stay with them.

30 It was as he reclined at the table with them that he took the bread, blessed and broke it, and gave it to them. 31 Then their eyes were opened, and they recognized him, but he disappeared from their sight. 32 They said to each other, "Weren't our hearts burning within us while he was talking with us on the road and explaining the Scriptures to us?" 33 That very hour they got up and returned to Jerusalem. They found the Eleven and those with them gathered together, 34 who said, "The Lord has truly been raised and has appeared to Simon!" 35 Then they began to describe what had happened on the road and how he was made known to them in the breaking of the bread.

THE REALITY OF THE RISEN JESUS

36 As they were saying these things, he himself stood in their midst. He said to them, "Peace to you!" 37 But they were startled and terrified and thought they were seeing a ghost. 38 "Why are you troubled?" he asked them. "And why do doubts arise in your hearts? 39 Look at my hands and my feet, that it is I myself! Touch me and see, because a ghost does not have flesh and bones as you can see I have." 40 Having said this, he showed them his hands and feet. 41 But while they still were amazed and in disbelief because of their joy, he asked them, "Do you have anything here to eat?" 42 So they gave him a piece of a broiled fish, 43 and he took it and ate in their presence.

44 He told them, "These are my words that I spoke to you while I was still with you—that everything written about me in the Law of Moses, the Prophets, and the Psalms must be fulfilled." 45 Then he opened their minds to understand the Scriptures. 46 He also said to them, "This is what is written: The Messiah will suffer and rise from the dead the third day, 47 and repentance for forgiveness of sins will be proclaimed in his name to all the nations, beginning at Jerusalem. 48 You are witnesses of these things. 49 And look, I am sending you what my Father promised. As for you, stay in the city until you are empowered from on high."

♥ GOING DEEPER

PSALM 16:9-11

9 Therefore my heart is glad
and my whole being rejoices;
my body also rests securely.
10 For you will not abandon me to Sheol;
you will not allow your faithful one to see decay.
11 You reveal the path of life to me;
in your presence is abundant joy;
at your right hand are eternal pleasures.

Response

PRAISE

During this Lenten season, we have taken time to lament—to grieve our own sin and express sorrow over the brokenness of the world, to which our sin contributes. As you think back on this week's Holy Week readings, use the space on the following page to reflect on the gift of salvation given through the life, death, and resurrection of Jesus. Write a prayer of praise thanking God for this gift.

BENEDICTION

"My dwelling place will be with them; I will be their God, and they will be my people."

EZEKIEL 37:27

Tips for Memorizing Scripture

At She Reads Truth, we believe Scripture memorization is an important discipline in your walk with God. Committing God's Truth to memory means He can minister to us—and we can minister to others—through His Word no matter where we are. As you approach the Weekly Truth passage in this book, try these memorization tips to see which techniques work best for you!

STUDY IT

Study the passage in its biblical context and ask yourself a few questions before you begin to memorize it: What does this passage say? What does it mean? How would I say this in my own words? What does it teach me about God? Understanding what the passage means helps you know why it is important to carry it with you wherever you go.

Break the passage into smaller sections, memorizing a phrase at a time.

PRAY IT

Use the passage you are memorizing as a prompt for prayer.

WRITE IT

Dedicate a notebook to Scripture memorization and write the passage over and over again.

Diagram the passage after you write it out. Place a square around the verbs, underline the nouns, and circle any adjectives or adverbs. Say the passage aloud several times, emphasizing the verbs as you repeat it. Then do the same thing again with the nouns, then the adjectives and adverbs.

Write out the first letter of each word in the passage somewhere you can reference it throughout the week as you work on your memorization.

Use a whiteboard to write out the passage. Erase a few words at a time as you continue to repeat it aloud. Keep erasing parts of the passage until you have it all committed to memory.

CREATE

If you can, make up a tune for the passage to sing as you go about your day, or try singing it to the tune of a favorite song.

Sketch the passage, visualizing what each phrase would look like in the form of a picture. Or, try using calligraphy or altering the style of your handwriting as you write it out.

Use hand signals or signs to come up with associations for each word or phrase and repeat the movements as you practice.

SAY IT

Repeat the passage out loud to yourself as you are going through the rhythm of your day—getting ready, pouring your coffee, waiting in traffic, or making dinner.

Listen to the passage read aloud to you.

Record a voice memo on your phone and listen to it throughout the day or play it on an audio Bible.

SHARE IT

Memorize the passage with a friend, family member, or mentor. Spontaneously challenge each other to recite the passage, or pick a time to review your passage and practice saying it from memory together.

Send the passage as an encouraging text to a friend, testing yourself as you type to see how much you have memorized so far.

KEEP AT IT!

Set reminders on your phone to prompt you to practice your passage.

Purchase a She Reads Truth 12 Card Set or keep a stack of notecards with Scripture you are memorizing by your bed. Practice reciting what you've memorized previously before you go to sleep, ending with the passages you are currently learning. If you wake up in the middle of the night, review them again instead of grabbing your phone. Read them out loud before you get out of bed in the morning.

Download the free Weekly Truth lock screens for your phone on the She Reads Truth app and read the passage throughout the day when you check your phone.

CSB BOOK ABBREVIATIONS

OLD TESTAMENT

GN Genesis

EX Exodus

LV Leviticus

NM Numbers

DT Deuteronomy

JOS Joshua

JDG Judges

RU Ruth

1SM 1 Samuel

2SM 2 Samuel

1KG 1 Kings

2KG 2 Kings

1CH 1 Chronicles

2CH 2 Chronicles

EZR Ezra

NEH Nehemiah

EST Esther

JB Job

PS Psalms

PR Proverbs

EC Ecclesiastes

SG Song of Solomon

IS Isaiah

JR Jeremiah

LM Lamentations

EZK Ezekiel

DN Daniel

HS Hosea

JL Joel

AM Amos

OB Obadiah

JNH Jonah

MC Micah

NAH Nahum

HAB Habakkuk

ZPH Zephaniah

HG Haggai

ZCH Zechariah

MAL Malachi

NEW TESTAMENT

MT Matthew

MK Mark

LK Luke

JN John

AC Acts

RM Romans

1CO 1 Corinthians

2CO 2 Corinthians

GL Galatians

EPH Ephesians

PHP Philippians

COL Colossians

1TH 1 Thessalonians

2TH 2 Thessalonians

1TM 1 Timothy

2TM 2 Timothy

TI Titus

PHM Philemon

HEB Hebrews

JMS James

1PT 1 Peter

2PT 2 Peter

1JN 1 John

2JN 2 John

3JN 3 John

JD Jude

RV Revelation

BIBLIOGRAPHY

Jenni, Ernst, and Claus Westermann. *Theological Lexicon of the Old Testament.* Peabody: Hendrickson Publishers, 1997.

Cooper, Lamar Eugene. *Ezekiel.* Vol. 17. The New American Commentary. Nashville: Broadman & Holman Publishers, 1994.

SHE READS TRUTH | BIBLE

Inspired by the She Reads Truth mission of "Women in the Word of God every day," the *She Reads Truth Bible* is thoughtfully and artfully designed to highlight the beauty, goodness, and truth found in Scripture.

FEATURES

- Custom reading plans to help you navigate your time in the Word

- Thoughtful devotionals throughout each book of the Bible

- Maps, charts, and timelines to provide context and Scripture connections

- 66 hand-lettered key verses to aid in Scripture memorization

USE CODE SRTB15 FOR
15% OFF YOUR NEW
SHE READS TRUTH BIBLE!

SHOPSHEREADSTRUTH.COM

You just spent 49 days in the Word of God!

MY FAVORITE DAY OF
THIS READING PLAN:

ONE THING I LEARNED
ABOUT GOD:

WHAT WAS GOD DOING IN
MY LIFE DURING THIS STUDY?

HOW DID I FIND DELIGHT IN GOD'S WORD?

WHAT DID I LEARN THAT I WANT TO SHARE
WITH SOMEONE ELSE?

A SPECIFIC SCRIPTURE THAT
ENCOURAGED ME:

A SPECIFIC SCRIPTURE THAT
CHALLENGED AND CONVICTED ME: